Praise for Opening to L

"Finally - a demystification of channeling! Jamye Price has pegged it! A person who is in channel is simply a person who has expanded consciousness. Within that expansion is art, music, sculpture...and an elegant 'Light Language.'

Opening to Light Language is a full explanation of how we can open up to our spiritual nature, and let go of old paradigms that say it can't be happening.

This truly is the next step, and a new piece of a profound multidimensional puzzle, which Kryon has predicted would be taught in the new energy past 2012. Congratulations Jamye, for being in the right place at the right time with this book!"

—**Lee Carroll Ph.D**, *original Channel for KRYON.* **www.kryon.com**

"Jamye is a beautiful teacher and leader in the field of sound and Light Language. She reminds us that we are all capable of speaking this Language. Articulate and insightful, she shares her multidimensional abilities in a spirit of true humility and respect. I adore reading and listening to her, she is a true evolutionary!"

—**Peggy Phoenix Dubro**, *originator of the EMF Balancing Technique, International teacher recognized in the field of energy psychology worldwide.* **www.thebalancingwork.com**

Get your free Light Language download at JamyePrice.com/what-is-light-language/

"For all those seeking personal empowerment, and overcoming the limitations of the mind, a transcendent roadmap has been offered. In Opening to Light Language, Jamye Price provides the background and method to dive within and hear and see the light of the divine that radiates naturally from you.

Intentionally pursuing the Language of Light can be viewed as a perceptual accelerator. For those who are ready to immerse themselves in the experience, a world of intuition and inspiration can be opened and revealed."

—**Todd Ovokaitys, MD,** *founder of Gematria Products, Inc., combining advanced nutritional formulas with a patented, time-reversed laser technology proven to improve the condition of many previously irreversible diseases. Dr. Todd Ovokaitys' work has been recognized worldwide as his products have reduced the effects of HIV, heart disease, aging, and more.* **www.Gematria.com**

"Opening to Light Language offers excellent information about the quantum telepathic Language of Light.

Jamye helps us understand this important gift, which communicates high-frequency information at a deeper level than can be conveyed by our linear language based upon externally agreed-upon concepts.

A highly recommended read for anyone who wants more knowledge of an intuitive heart and soul experience that is difficult to explain."

—**Yvonne Perry,** *author of Light Language Emerging ~ Activating Ascension Codes & Integrating Body, Soul, & Spirit.* **http://weare1inspirit.com**

"Jamye Price shares within the pages of this book knowledge, wisdom, and practical applications that are valuable and very much needed as we each evolve during these ever elusive and fascinat-ing times. Over the years I've watched her facilitate and share her innate knowingness with grace—enhancing the lives of those who are willing and ready.

Jamye is the real deal. Yes, that sounds so clichéd, but it's the truth! She shows up to Life very human and completely grounded to Earth, yet she's connected to the multidimensional galaxies in a way that's mystifying and so compelling. As you read *Opening to Light Language*, you'll inevitably feel your own inherent connections enhanced, as well as gain greater insights and aptitudes to assist in your evolution."

—**Rebecca Joy,** *speaker, creator of the Simple Awareness Method (S.A.M.) and author of Classic Tales from the Firehouse: Firefighters' Stories of Calamity, Courage, and Caring.* **SimpleAwareness.com, TalesFromTheFirehouse.com**

Opening to Light Language

OPENING TO LIGHT LANGUAGE

HUMANITY'S EVOLUTION INTO MULTIDIMENSIONAL COMMUNICATION

JAMYE PRICE

Crystalline Soul Healing, LLC

Copyright © 2015 Crystalline Soul Healing, LLC

All rights reserved. No part of this publication may be used or reproduced in any form without the express permission of the author. No part of this book is intended to diagnose or cure any physical, mental, or emotional disease. It is for educational and informational purposes only.

Library of Congress Cataloging-in-Publication Data

Library of Congress Control Number: 2015915817
Price, Jamye 2015
Opening to Light Language: Humanity's Evolution into Multidimensional Communication, Jamye Price

ISBN: 978-0-9968586-0-1

Editors: Mary Holden, Leah Wohl-Pollack

Published in the United States by Crystalline Soul Healing, LLC

To Todd

Thank you for strengthening me and supporting me through this journey.

To my Soul Sister

I was shown true sisterhood through you. Thank you for walking beside me even when we are far away.

"And the day came when the risk to remain tight in a bud was more painful than the risk it took to blossom."

— Anaïs Nin

Learn Light Language online with Jamye.
Visit JamyePrice.com/how-to-learn-light-language/

Contents

Foreword
By Lyssa Royal Holt VIII
Preface XIII
Acknowledgments XV
Introduction XVII
    How to Read This Book xix
    Poetic License xx
    The Voice of This Book xxi

Jamye's Story
Chapter One
My Psychic Opening 3
    The Opening Begins 4
    The Opening Increases 5
    Empathic Pain 6
    Spirituality Surfaces 9
    Healing Begins 12
    Another Psychic Opening Phase 15

Chapter Two
Light Language Arises 18
    Light Language Grows 22
    Taming the Fear 26
    Final Steps Begin 31
    Gentle Growth Continues 36
    Light Language Expands 41

What is Light Language?
Chapter Three
Overview of Light Language 47
    Multidimensional Language 49

Why Now? 52
The Nature of the Unknown 54
Do No Harm 56
Profound Change 59
Sacred Communication 61

Chapter Four
Energy, Frequency, and Vibration 63
Frequency 65
Resonance 67
The Power of Perception 68

Chapter Five
The Quantum Nature of Light 72
Wave or Particle Light 73
Holographic Reality 74

Chapter Six
Sacred Geometry 78
Masculine Energy and Feminine Energy 80

Chapter Seven
The Alchemy of Sound 87
The Visible Effects of Sound 88
The Emotional Effects of Sound 90

Chapter Eight
The Evolution of Language 92
Creative Word 93
Language Origins 94
Valuable Separation 95
Written Communication 97
Connective Language 99
Transitioning Beyond Linear Language 100
Speaking in Tongues 102
Quantum Language 104
Telepathic Communication 105
Humanity Evolves 107

MULTIDIMENSIONAL LIFE

CHAPTER NINE

OVERVIEW OF MULTIDIMENSIONALITY 111
- Density or Dimension? 113
- Lower and Higher Dimensions 114
- Multidimensional Progression 116

CHAPTER TEN

THE DIMENSIONS 118
- You Are Multidimensional 120
- Multidimensional Awareness 128

CHAPTER ELEVEN

ASCENSION 132
- The Yugas 135
- Reunification 136
- Evolution 138

CHAPTER TWELVE

LIGHT LANGUAGE AND DNA 142
- DNA and Light 144
- Invisible Connection 146
- DNA Activation 148

CHAPTER THIRTEEN

THE HIGHER SELF 151
- Communicating with Your Higher Self 153
- Creating Your Reality 154
- Soul Progression for Ascension 156

CHAPTER FOURTEEN

THE HEART 157
- Your Emotional Signals 158
- The Emotions of Ascension 159
- Resolving Emotional Imbalance 160
- Neutral Observance 162
- Healing Emotions 165
- Creating with Emotions 166

Empowered Love	167
Language of the Heart	168

Chapter Fifteen
The Brain — 170
Valuable Data	172
Expanding the Mind	174
Your Brain, Your Choice	175

Chapter Sixteen
The Ego — 178
The Beneficial Ego	179
Balancing the Ego	181
Embracing Change	183

Chapter Seventeen
Intent — 185
The Courage to Look Within	187
Recognizing Intent	189
Healthy Intent	191

Types of Light Language

Chapter Eighteen
Overview of Light Language Categories — 197
Light Language Origins	198

Chapter Nineteen
Elven Light Language — 202
Elven Elementals	204
Life Sciences	206
Elven Interaction since Lyra	206
Elven Wisdom	208
Elven Influence	209

Chapter Twenty
Faerie Light Language — 212
Faerie Joy	213
Human Faeries	214

Faerie Work	215
Faerie Fun	217

Chapter Twenty One
Angelic Light Language — 218
Protecting and Serving	220
Angelic Connection	222

Chapter Twenty Two
Galactic Light Language — 224
Starseed History	225
Galactic Communication	227

Channeling Light Language

Chapter Twenty Three
Overview of Channeling — 233
What Is Channeling?	234
Barriers to Channeling	236
Channeling with Safety	237
A Foundation of Trust	239
Setting Pure Intent	240

Chapter Twenty Four
Opening to Channeling Light Language — 243
Beginning Observation	245
Practicing Channeling Light Language	247

Chapter Twenty Five
Finding Your Voice — 251
Recognizing Light Language	252
Beginning with Light Language	253
Practice Is Imperative	256

Chapter Twenty Six
Moving the Energy — 258
Let it Flow Slowly	260

CHAPTER TWENTY SEVEN	
WRITING THE ENERGY	263
Writing Light Language	265
CHAPTER TWENTY EIGHT	
TRANSLATING LIGHT LANGUAGE	268
Observing Sensory Data	270
Pay Attention with Ease	271
CHAPTER TWENTY NINE	
HEALING WITH LIGHT LANGUAGE	273
Finding Your Path	274
How to Heal with Light Language	274
Trusting Your Path	275
Enjoying Your Path	277
CHAPTER THIRTY	
REPRESENTING LIGHT LANGUAGE	279
Your Self-Respect and Courage	280
Consideration of Others	281
Healing Ego Imbalances	283
Sacred Flow	285

UNIVERSAL NATURE

CHAPTER THIRTY ONE	
THE FIRST PATH	289
CHAPTER THIRTY TWO	
THE SECOND PATH	293
CHAPTER THIRTY THREE	
THE THIRD PATH	299
CONCLUSION	302
GLOSSARY	305
BIBLIOGRAPHY	317

Foreword

By Lyssa Royal Holt

It is surprising that in my thirty years of channeling (and very often working with cosmic and/or extraterrestrial energies) that my first experience with Light Language happened only in 2009. Since then, I have seen the incidences of this universal communication increasing among my channeling students, without them even knowing what it is or having seen it before. To this day Light Language is still not very understood, even by those of us whose life's work has been in the field of channeling. For this reason, I am honored to have been asked by Jamye to write the foreword to this book because the work she is doing is helping to shed light on this fascinating, powerful, and often misunderstood phenomenon.

    I have been working steadily in Japan since 1990, offering workshops, channel trainings and private sessions. It is there, in 2009, that I had my first experience with Light Language. A student came to me for a private session. She was very confused. She was receiving a form of written communication that she didn't understand. The characters she was writing were consistent and they would come in short bursts. She felt guided to write these channelings on parchment. Her family (who didn't really believe in this sort of thing) became intrigued. She began to write the communications on dissolvable parchment and her family began dissolving them in their nightly baths. Her family said that they felt a noticeable healing affect from doing this, and that is when her life's work began.

In her private session with me, my channeled contacts told her that it was an ancient sacred language used in the Vega star system by priests and priestesses. They told her that the writings were prayers, which is why they had a healing effect. Though she doubted what she was doing, she kept doing it because of the response from her clients. I was greatly moved by these prayers and even took one of her dissolvable parchments to dissolve off the coast of Okinawa while doing sacred work with a group in 2010.

A few more years went by and suddenly, more students in my channeling classes began verbally channeling Light Language, even though I do not do it myself or teach others how to do it. The most recent experience with one of my students was a turning point in my understanding of this phenomenon. My student, an elder woman in her sixties, would channel this language during the channeling practice in my class. She became increasingly frustrated, however, because she could not understand the meaning and desperately wanted to do so. Just before her graduation, she came to me for a private session so that she could learn how to translate and understand what was coming to her.

I led her through a series of exercises and then something unexpected happened—she spontaneously remembered a traumatic past life in ancient Greece when her entire family was killed. She was alone and desperate. She called out to the universe and an intelligence came to her, embraced her, and promised it would not leave her. She was sobbing as she recalled this and suddenly understood that the energy she was channeling now was this same intelligence. As we did more exercises together, a profound integration happened. She began to be able to translate the Light Language that was coming to her. Somehow, the release of the trauma she had been carrying created an integration in her psyche—almost like connecting a plug to a source of energy that she couldn't access before. If she hadn't engaged the process of using this language (even when she did not understand it), she never would have had the healing experience that moved her to the next level of her development.

This doesn't mean that if Light Language is not able to be translated, then it is due to a past trauma. Instead, it supports the philosophy behind how I teach channeling. If taught in a certain way, channeling can be a profound process of inner integration and spiritual development. Channeling can take many forms. Just like verbal channeling in a known Earth language, Light Language channeling can be a way to also begin the process of inner integration needed to move to a next step in human evolution—as long as it isn't used to escape any pain that is stored in one's psyche. (One of my students actually admitted to using Light Language to avoid dealing with human beings. Obviously, this is not recommended!)

The only other experience I've had with Light Language is with Jamye herself. In 2014 she was part of my annual Contact and Consciousness Retreat in Arizona. To make a long story short, it is well known amongst my students that a praying mantis often represents a specific ET group that I call the Founders. To simplify, they are a very high-frequency group that are quite far removed from physicality and really represent universal consciousness in its most pure form. Our group had felt their presence quite strongly during this retreat.

As our group arrived at our desert contact site on both nights, our praying mantis friend was waiting for us. We considered him a mascot of sorts and showered him with attention, which he loved. But the magic happened when Jamye began speaking Light Language to him. He jumped on her body, crawling all over her to rest on her crown chakra. It was as if he was having a love affair with her as she spoke Light Language to him. It was a touching and beautiful sight, and was quite obvious that he was responding to the Light Language. Being that the Founders are nonphysical and their frequency resides very close to the Universal One, a universal Light Language would be the most compatible form of communication between us. On that night, we all got to witness Jamye's ability to act as a conduit between worlds through Light Language.

We are fortunate to have human guides on Earth to help us remember and reconnect with the more universal aspects of our consciousness through books such as this. As you read this book, allow the information to trigger an opening that goes much deeper than the mind. As you resonate with the material, an internal unfolding begins. Follow the thread, even into the unknown. You will find that the journey always leads you back to your true essence—pure consciousness itself.

—Lyssa Royal Holt
Author of *The Prism of Lyra, Preparing for Contact, and the Galactic Heritage Cards.*
www.lyssaroyal.net

Preface

I never expected that my life would take such an unusual path. I did not easily recognize that something so seemingly odd would turn out to be my greatest teacher. I resisted sharing Light Language for many years because I felt I would be giving up a normal life. The fear of being judged by others, as well as my own internal judgments, held me back. At first, I didn't even feel comfortable speaking it aloud by myself.

Through the Language of Light, I began experiencing such a profound communion with Life that I eventually felt compelled to share it with the world. What I found is a new normal—one that contains a deep inner connection with the loving, invisible world that surrounds us. For this reason, I choose to share the experience of Light Language with you.

In this book you will discover what Light Language is and how it may have a positive effect on you and others, if that is a path you choose. You will learn some of the esoteric information humanity is yearning to embody and science is beginning to confirm.

It is my hope that as you understand my fears, resistance, excitement, and ultimate surrender into a greater experience of Life through Light Language, you will open your heart to your own unique path. Every being brings a beautiful gift to this world. Often it is hidden beneath fear and only revealed through the courage of Love. I found my courage with determination and passion that kept me moving forward. Most importantly, I found Loving support from others until I learned to Love and support myself as well. Reach out to Life. The world becomes a better place.

Acknowledgments

A deep thank you to my partner Todd for supporting me through a weird journey to a new normal. I love you so much. Mom and Dad, for not being too surprised when I spontaneously erupted into Light Language on the couch. My soul sister, who arrived just as things were getting a little too weird to handle. My (anonymous) Artist Friend, for showing me heart, talent, and so many cool upgrades. My soul brother for unconditional love and support—just wow. Margaret Dellinger, for making this wealth of experience so fun—you still make me want to sing. Kevin Gaspard, for never giving up on my growth and pushing it to new levels. Karen Kolczak, for continually supporting and balancing me into greater clarity—you are a gem. Rebecca Joy, for constant inspiration; breathing life in deeply with you is always worth it. Lyssa Royal Holt, for being so kind and supportive. Right when I needed to see the embodiment of integrity and talent, you appeared. Lee Carroll, for work that has been a touchstone in my growth and for bringing many of these people into my life.

Thank you to my wonderful editors and readers that made this book so much better: Mary Holden, Leah Wohl-Pollack, and Lynn Louise Wonders, as well as many of the aforementioned.

A huge thank you to my clients. You have amazed me with your courage and I am blessed to meet you. I thank you so much for the sacred trust you put in me. My life is forever changed as I witness your magnificence which is often hidden within. I am honored to help you see your Light. Eeshah, Ehmah, Ehtah.

Introduction

You were drawn to this book for a reason. As one interested in Light Language and its possibilities in your life, you are part of a blooming expansion that is occurring as humanity's communication becomes more authentic and connective. This book is a comprehensive study of the Language of Light and its effects on humanity. It goes much deeper into the quantum nature of Light Language than when I teach others to transmit it, because my class is highly experiential. The Language of Light is a vast subject with many implications for the multidimensional opening humanity is experiencing.

    This book isn't an easy read. It will stir questions and changes in perception. It will bring esoteric topics into applicable, detailed understanding. As you read this book, you are receiving information and energy imprints as appropriate for you *through the filter of your Higher Self.* This will help you understand the information on a deeper level, though that may unfold over time. Always use your discernment of what feels right to you, yet keep an open mind to new information so you can adjust as you deem necessary.

The term "light language" or "the language of light" has been applied to variations of expression that may not refer to genuine language communication. In this book, I am discussing actual language that is being communicated, even though most people don't understand the words or the depth of energy transmitted along with it. If we spoke very broadly, everything is language because information is always being transmitted, even in silence. But to have a deeper understanding and not create unconscious avoidance of the applicability of the vast into the linear, we must journey from linear to the next level of connection and the next.

This book is referring to speaking real—though unknown (unless you can translate the Light Language)—Languages that initiate a deep, cellular change in the listener. In actuality, everything creates light, as light is a response to electromagnetic movement (waves) and carries information. Even if you hold your breath, don't move and don't think; you are still emitting light as your cellular structure creates movement.

When you speak aloud, you are creating light with your words. *However, speaking a language you consciously know utilizes your brain in different ways and creates a different response in the listener than Light Language does.* I discovered this intuitively from the comparison of channeling in a language I know versus Light Language. When I channel in English, I cannot use my brain in the same way I do with Light Language. If I pay attention too much, or begin to think my own thoughts in response to the English channeling, I inhibit the flow of the information. This is because when I channel in English, my known vocabulary is being utilized by the energy I am channeling.

When one channels Light Language, the brain is not choosing from known, memorized and contextualized words. The Language of Light is not as linear and pre-defined as our known languages. Therefore, the parts of the brain used when transmitting Light Language are different because it is a non-linear, unmemorized and uncontextualized flow of information. It does not activate the frontal lobe in the way that speaking a known language does.[1]

How to Read This Book

If this subject matter is entirely new to you, please glance through the glossary first. Because of the substantial subject matter in this book, I recommend you read it from start to finish once. In the beginning you may not fully understand a term that seems to be casually thrown into a sentence. It is likely detailed in a later chapter, or at the very least it may be defined in the glossary. At times, you'll notice minor repetition as I associate topics or encourage a broader comprehension. The flow of information is designed to help you build a foundational understanding of how deeply Light Language affects your life.

This book is organized by chapters that fall into six categories. The first section relays my personal opening to the Language of Light to help you better understand my experience. The second section will lay a foundation of the quantum implications of Light Language as it applies to life and humanity as a whole. The third section will relate it to your personal evolution through your multidimensional

---

1 University of Pennsylvania preliminary SPECT study (Newberg, Wintering, Morgan, Waldman)

nature. The fourth section teaches the overarching types of Light Language, while the fifth section offers exercises to begin a practice of opening to it—if you so choose. In the final section I discuss humanity's universal nature, of which the Language of Light may be one small aspect; moving the fractal focus into the greater expanse.

Once you have read through the entire book, you may want to re-read certain chapters so that as you begin to practice, you are reminded of their depth and application along the way. This can help you feel more confident experimenting with something so new. If you desire a more personal teaching of Light Language, you can visit my website, JamyePrice.com, to determine if a class is right for you.

Poetic License

You will find certain words capitalized that do not follow proper grammatical structure. I've done this intentionally to denote that a word or phrase has a broader meaning than what is normally defined. For example, when "Life" is capitalized, it refers to the broad collective of Life—all beings, consciousness, universal laws, and experiences that are contained within Life as a whole. When it is not capitalized, it is the conventional understanding of the human experience without the full implication of the collective and cosmic connection. When "Language" is capitalized, it refers to the many Languages of Light. Without capitalization, language means our normal, spoken human languages.

> *Light Language bridges the unknown of the defining intellect with the known of the unifying heart.*

It is important to establish a clear understanding of how "transmitting" and "receiving" Light Language are discussed in this book. It is a process of channeling, so one is always receiving when Light Language is coming through their voice, hands, or body. For clarity, I will refer to transmitting Light Language as coming through you and out into the physical world (even if no one else is there). Receiving it refers to when someone else is transmitting it to you. For example, if you watch one of my Light Language videos,[1] I am transmitting and you are receiving. This is how I refer to it throughout the book, although I am technically receiving (channeling) even as I transmit.

To clarify further, to "translate" Light Language refers to interpreting the meaning of the transmission. It does not refer to translating the frequencies into written, verbal, or movement form. While that is technically happening, for agreement of terms, I call that transmitting.

THE VOICE OF THIS BOOK

Light Language inherently begins a more conceptual opening of communication. *It bridges the unknown of the defining intellect with the known of the unifying*

---

1 JamyePrice.com/videos

heart. This book, in keeping with that bridge, will follow some unconventional paths to understanding, both in voice and context.

The voice of this book will follow a teaching structure, for it is like a textbook with a less formal constitution of teaching. Just as the advent of YouTube began to break down the third wall of separation between audience and presenter, I want this book to feel more like how I prefer to teach. At times the tone will be presentational—more removed so you will be more mentally involved and begin to conceptualize. It may quickly change to a more personal tense and tone as I shift between me, you, and us. This conversational change helps you empathize and apply information into your life more readily. I believe it is important to adopt a fluid structure as we journey into the expansion of communication through the vehicle of Light Language.

My logical mind has always continued to seek a context for the understanding of Light Language, not just for the sounds and shapes themselves (which comes naturally to me), but also for the need of my life to change so drastically. This adjustment to something so unusual surfacing in my life is the reason I chose to teach the Language of Light to students from around the world. I am honored to assist those who are adjusting to or drawn to such an unconventional experience. I wish for others to have access to the expansion, connection, and evolution I have received from my experience with the Language of Light.

It is important to keep in mind that the context of this book cannot yet be fully proven by our current scientific methods. I am writing from my personal experience of over a decade of working directly with the Language of Light. As an empathic, clairaudient channel, much of this is intuitive information I received from my team of Guides, which are not in physical form. I expound from years of working with others who opened to Light Language before there was easy access to information about it. I communicate from discovery with clients who trusted my peculiar way of working to help them along their paths.

Light Language belongs to the subtle realms, where the quantum nature of information is less structured and more malleable by perception (observation) and intent.

The current scientific structure is valuable, but it is limited. The ability to define proof through mathematics or by recreating an experiment applies well to Newtonian physics. *Light Language belongs to the subtle realms, bridging the non-linear; where the quantum nature of information is less structured and more malleable by perception (observation) and intent.* Therefore, I will correlate it to newer scientific models that are not as universally agreed upon.

Though Light Language is more conceptual than the languages we use to communicate, I implore you to trust your own wise discernment of what you feel resonates as truth for you. Don't just take my word for it. Experience it. Keep an open mind. Question things. Hone your discernment. Use a system like muscle testing or a pendulum until you grow your confidence. Find your internal wisdom. This wisdom is innate to humanity, but it hasn't necessarily been nurtured into valuable strength and openness. This changes as we each learn to cultivate our own internal wisdom.

Here we begin to plant some wisdom seeds with Light Language and watch humanity grow.

SECTION ONE

Light Language: Coming of Age

Jamye's Story

The purpose of the following section is to help you frame how intuitive senses can open and affect your life, as well as Light Language specifically. I loved energy healing and felt a deep passion for it, but as soon as Light Language started opening up, I hid and resisted for many years. My hope is that this story will help you feel comfortable with your unique path, even if it doesn't involve Light Language.

Chapter One

My Psychic Opening

I wasn't psychic as a child, but I was generally a quiet and sensitive child—the youngest of two half-siblings that were six and seven years older. My parents worked diligently to provide all we needed, but the physical, emotional, and mental atmosphere I experienced from my half-siblings was beyond the control of my parents.

From the environment in my home I learned that it was safest to step back, stay quiet, and watch the world proceed. The easiest place to live was in my imagination. I was an introvert, perhaps by survival, though at the time I did not have a concept of my sensitivity.

As a child, I did not have any conscious experiences of psychic phenomena or any extraterrestrial visitations. I have been told by multiple people that I had a visitation experience when I was younger and they all mention the exact same age—six years old. I still do not recall any visitation experience and I have no symptoms of any sort of abduction. While I have always felt drawn to the stars, I have never had any fear of extraterrestrials, so clearly the experience was positive.

In general, my teen years were fine. I thrived when I was outside of my home environment. I graduated a year early from high school because I could not wait to get out of the house and my small town.

The Opening Begins

When I went to college at seventeen, I began having odd recurring daydreams. I wondered why I would think such horrible things compulsively. Finally, I talked to my half-sister about these perplexing daydreams and she told me they were memories of things that had really happened.

I was surprised to learn I had dissociated memories to deal with trauma, because at that point in my life I felt like such a strong person. I did not realize how sensitive I was because I shut that part of myself down to deal with the trauma of my home environment. Around the same time I would get depressed for no apparent reason, but it would pass after a few days.

I studied modern dance in college. Dancing was just about the only thing that I loved; being on a stage dancing or acting. Dance was a safe zone of expression for me.

My first out-of-body experience occurred while I was performing an improvisational dance piece. I suddenly found myself experiencing tunnel vision as the entire room became cloudy. Then I was slightly above my body, watching the performance. It was an exhilarating feeling to be above my body and watch it move. I was still cognizant, just not in my normal way. I didn't have any reference for what was happening, but I enjoyed it.

This time in my life brought many openings. Some were difficult, like memories resurfacing and depression, while others were interesting, like the out-of-body experience. I also had two strong past-life memories in college. I didn't know how or why, since I had no exposure to teachings of reincarnation in my small Southern town, but it was clear to me these were past-life memories.

My psychic senses were beginning to open, though I couldn't control them. At this point, the experience of a psychic phenomenon was a rare occurrence, perhaps a few times a year.

The Opening Increases

After college, in the early 1990s, I started experiencing more psychic phenomena that would be proven correct within a few hours. They usually occurred while I was driving, as rote activity is mildly hypnotic and sometimes initiates a brainwave pattern that is more open.

As I was driving, I would have a flash of someone I knew who was going to be where I was going. It was always an unusual circumstance, such as someone I hadn't seen or perhaps even thought of in years. It was usually a place I would not expect to see that person, too—once it was even in a different state (within the United States), far from home!

The information came in a spoken thought form that seemed like mine, though it was impossible for me to have been thinking about it. It would happen so fast: "Susan is going to be there." I always assumed I'd just had a random thought, until it was proven true every time. I did not even know it was possible to receive thought impulses as a psychic sense.

For about five years, my psychic abilities slowly grew, though I was typically unaware of them.

Empathic Pain

In the mid-1990s I moved to Los Angeles to pursue a career in acting. I loved dance, but I needed a steady income after college and I could hardly subsist as a modern dancer. I focused more on acting and followed my dreams to California, where I had wanted to move since I was young. I felt much more at home in the big city than I did in the South.

I took Method acting classes, which I loved because The Method focused on sense memory and exploring emotions. I had naturally worked that way even before taking acting classes. Studying theatre was a way for me to explore my own emotions and allow them to flow through a character on a stage. I knew it was helpful, but not enough to heal me, because my depression was increasing and enduring.

I had never been to a psychic, but when a particular psychic came highly recommended, I decided to try it. I noticed that when I left her house, the inside of my face was tingling. My eyes, my sinuses, and the inside of my forehead itched. While it seemed like I was having an allergic reaction, it felt slightly different. I didn't know what to make of it.

As I was driving home from her house, I saw a mother walking her baby in a stroller. She was too far away to discern any sort of facial expression and she looked completely non-descript. However, my response to her shocked me. I felt a wave of emotional pain so strong that I instantly thought, "I have to close myself, I can't handle it!" The thought was an immediate and urgent response.

I had no idea about empathic capabilities, or even what "closing myself" meant, but just being around the psychic had opened me up. It wasn't until many years later that I realized I had shut down as a child in an atmosphere of intense emotional pressure. The opening was happening naturally because I had left the harmful environment.

The psychic had just sped it up.

At this time, the depression that began in college was becoming more frequent and lasting for longer periods. There was no rhyme or reason to it; as I did not have such a challenging life to warrant this deep depression. Yet it grew from an occasional three days of malaise into an average of three weeks of severe depression with perhaps one week of normalcy per month. Feeling normal was not much relief. I felt I had no control over my emotions and spent the time I wasn't depressed worried about feeling depressed again.

I was waiting tables in Los Angeles, and sometimes I could not hold back the tears. I would face the wall and pretend I was looking at the orders in my book while I cried. No one knew what was going on within me. My depression was turning into thoughts of suicide. More than anything, I wanted to get away from the unexplained and uncontrollable pain so badly that I felt death would be the only relief. I would work through different pros and cons of suicide plans, but there was always one catch—what to do with my beloved cat. I could handle everything except that detail, because any mention of giving my cat away to someone would raise suspicion. I wasn't about to get so close to what I thought would be relief, and then get blocked by some well-meaning person who didn't understand the pain I was experiencing.

I did not have a lot of trust in the systems I knew of, such as psychology and allopathic medicine. I hated life at this point, so taking a pill to endure it only to have different challenges from side effects was not appealing. But since a suicide plan wasn't working out, I finally did reach out for help. I casually mentioned my depression to a co-worker I barely knew. I wouldn't normally have spoken to him (or almost anyone) about something so personal. I now realize it was a soul prompting.

The emotional aspect was causing a physical reaction in my body that created a chemical (hormonal) overwhelm.

He suggested reflexology based on his personal experience. Reflexology is foot massage that works like acupuncture to move energy through the physical system. This felt right to me, so I decided to give it a try. I went for treatment once a week for three months and took some herbs that were prescribed. The reflexology was incredibly painful; I squirmed and cried, but endured. I soon began feeling better.

The reflexologist confirmed that there was a chemical imbalance causing the depression. I agree. I also know now that the chemical imbalance was caused by repressed emotions surfacing because I was no longer in the stressful environment of my half-siblings. The emotional aspect, although it was running in the background rather than occurring as a reaction to my current experience, was causing a physical reaction in my body that created a chemical (hormonal) overwhelm. Reflexology helped me get my physical/chemical body back in line. I now had the presence of mind to deal with the negative mental chatter I was noticing.

Spirituality Surfaces

Now that I was feeling more stable, I could connect with friends and life again. One of my friends introduced me to Jamie Sam's Sacred Path Cards and book. I noticed I could see white light around certain cards and I felt a quick tug of energy when my hand was over the card I should choose. I enjoyed the information in the book even more than the cards, as I recognized truths in it: honor all life, observe your motivations, treat yourself and others with kindness and respect. I finally found something that felt right to me. These weren't rules to keep people or God from judging me as right or wrong, they were internal tools to learn to honor others as well as myself.

Along with my first exposure to spiritual concepts, my psychic senses increased at a rapid pace. I had multiple experiences of waking up as my legs were being held down by a ghost. This happened a few times within a month, which was really uncomfortable and scary!

Finally, when I awoke being held down again, I wondered in my mind, "What is this about?" I was shocked to get an answer! I immediately had a vision of a soldier talking to me. He told me he had died many years ago. The building where I worked was now built over the place where he had died. He showed me the exact spot, which now had a large piece of furniture on it. I asked him why he was telling me this and he said he just wanted me to know. I never heard from him again and I was never held down again.

This was my first exposure to an earthbound entity, though not my last. A few years later, my boyfriend and I went to a house in the mountains to meet some friends. We got there at night and had a fun time hanging out with everyone. I awoke abruptly in the middle of the night. As I opened my eyes, I saw an old man standing in the corner of the room, looking at me. I knew he was a ghost. He looked like a figure of dim light, but I could see his features well enough to determine that he was old. I didn't know what to do.

I didn't feel I was in danger, like in a scary movie, but I didn't feel comfortable either. I thought, "I wonder if I needed my Nanny, would she come help me?" My great-grandmother, whom I called Nanny, had died about fifteen years earlier. As soon as I had the thought, I felt her at the foot of the bed and she zoomed up beside my head so she was standing between me and the other ghost. I couldn't see her, but I felt her location and energy acutely. I couldn't see the old man any more either.

I went back to sleep knowing Nanny was standing beside me, watching over me, in ethereal form. The next morning I woke up and went into the kitchen to get coffee. This was the first time I had seen the surrounding area in daylight. A graveyard was across the street. I knew with certainty that this was where the old man had come from. This was a pivotal experience for me because I learned I could ask for help if an entity was bothering me. It's a little mystifying to me how I managed to remain so calm during all of this, though the experiential teachings about holding boundaries were helpful.

During this time I learned many lessons that were beginning to build a foundation of knowledge for me. I also occasionally saw people's auras, mostly in my mind's eye, though I didn't know anything about the aura at that time. I saw light and colors around people, as well as energy reaching out from them and connecting to others. I would see some people joined at different chakra points, though I didn't know details about the chakras. I had no idea what to do with the information, but I was enthralled with this new area of discovery that was opening in my life.

HEALING BEGINS

In the mid- and late 1990s, thoughts about subjects I knew nothing about began to come into my mind. I remember one time in particular, I found myself "thinking" about the healing properties of the color green. It was as if I had been zoned out, then became aware that I was hearing my thoughts speaking a discourse on the subject. I had never been exposed to the concept of the healing properties of colors, so I had no reference for this occurrence. I thought it was odd I was even thinking such thoughts. I assumed I was daydreaming. What I did not know at the time was that I was receiving thought impulses from my Guides and Higher Self.

One day, before I had ever been exposed to any sort of energy healing, I awoke feeling like I was getting the flu. I had the impulse to slowly run my hand about an inch above my body. To my surprise, I found some places felt hot to my psychic senses. In my mind's eye, I saw a grey cloud moving from a "hot spot" in my body into my hand. I found this fascinating. I held my hand there until I didn't see the cloud in my mind's eye anymore, then lifted my palm to the sky and let my hand empty. I did this for a while then went back to sleep for an hour or so. I awoke feeling perfectly healthy—no sense of flu, no fatigue, nothing.

I repeated this process whenever I started feeling sick. I even did it on my boyfriend, family and friends when they were getting sick, but I didn't tell them I was doing it. I wasn't trying to be sneaky, I just wanted to help. Since I had no idea if it would work on them at first, I didn't tell them. It always worked. I even started using different visualizations, like a strong wind blowing through the entire body, or a laser beam of light going from the top of the head slowly down the body. Each time I tried it, it worked!

In the late 1990s, after a long Screen Actors Guild strike, acting opportunities were few and far between, so I decided to go to massage school. I find the physical body fascinating, and I had a good sense of the muscles and their pain from being a dancer. I went to a technical school where the instructors didn't talk much about energy. There was only one casual mention of grounding your energy before a massage.

> ***I received some outside validation; this is one way your Guides teach and speak with you.***

Once during class, however, the teacher advised us to put our hands an inch or so above the person's head, hold for about five seconds, then move our hands away. He was just teaching a technique for ending a massage, not giving us instructions on chakras. As I was receiving this technique from a fellow student, I felt my whole energy being squished and suppressed. It was uncomfortable. For some odd reason, my immediate thought was, "This is what it feels like to be with my boyfriend," with whom I was experiencing a tumultuous break-up. Then the massage student took her hands away and I felt myself expand taller. It felt wonderful. In that moment I was completely over my boyfriend. I was free from repression (my energy feeling suppressed), not just a relationship breaking up.

Soon after this experience I received some outside validation; this is one way your Guides teach and speak with you. I saw a fellow restaurant server who had always seen me in three-inch-high tennis shoes at work. I was wearing flat shoes, so I was three inches shorter than when he normally saw me. He said, "You look taller!" I was so surprised! I knew he was seeing the energetic version of me, rather than my physical being. On a soul level, he was responding to my energy field and fulfilling a call from my Higher Self to support and teach me. I was "taller" because my energy was no longer being suppressed. And of course, I was the one who had been letting it be suppressed by my boyfriend.

I did massage for about four years. I would sometimes get flashes of emotional trauma or past-life experiences from my massage clients. During this valuable time of learning through massage, I observed how the physical body related to the emotional body. I began to correlate people's emotional patterns with their physical habits. It was a fascinating study of the mind/body complex.

I still didn't know about my natural empathic abilities—I did not realize I was subconsciously taking people's challenges into my body during a massage. I began having anxiety attacks for the first time in my life, and they were always unprovoked. After about a year of occasional anxiety attacks, I recognized I was having them because other people's energy was overwhelming my system. It took me many years to stop taking people's energy into my body, and it's something I still continue to keep in check today.

Many people have unconscious (or conscious) past-life memories of being a healer during a time when the best way to heal was to take the other person's problem into you and heal it for them. We don't need to work this way anymore. It is safe to let it go and allow new healing modalities to arise. As a highly empathic person, I am now able to receive the data without taking on the energy. When I do healing work, I am experiencing physical, emotional, and mental information (as well as other psychic data) in my body, but I no longer allow another's energy into my body. I simply receive information.

At times, it may be physically uncomfortable. For instance, I may feel a gentle 'pain' in my liver which indicates a problem in their liver. Nothing has happened to my liver, no energy from that person is in my liver; my body is like a mirror reflecting information. The same thing happens with thoughts and emotions. After a session I feel invigorated because I have been in contact with immense Love during a session. That is what heals another, not my body.

Another Psychic Opening Phase

In the early 2000s, I experienced another increase in psychic phenomena. I now recognized conversations with my Guides. I heard angels sing during meditation. I was getting more detailed psychic information, and being taught profound esoteric information by my Guides. I was learning about empathy, protecting my energy field, and the value of forgiveness. I was accessing knowledge I didn't know I could have. During this time, I began doing my own healing work on willing friends and family, as I was being taught how to work on others by my Guides. I finally started reading some books about energy and was getting some more exposure now through massage friends.

At the end of 2002, I drove to Sedona, Arizona with a massage friend who did an Axiatonal Alignment on me. As he started, I felt strong, distinct physical sensations. I felt my hair blowing from incredibly fast hand movements above my head. The sensation was so specific that I knew the shape his fingers were making. Later I found out he was not doing anything like the movement I had sensed at all. He wasn't even moving around quickly. I was feeling someone else working.

Then I felt a finger on my forehead blazing rapidly up and down. Somehow I knew this was not my friend's finger. My eyes were closed, but I knew this finger was much longer than a human finger. I felt a few more sensations, then the next thing I knew I woke up, though I didn't open my eyes.

Based on my perception of time, I thought maybe fifteen minutes had passed, but it was actually over forty-five minutes. My forehead continued buzzing for our entire trip. My psychic senses began another potent opening, though there were no obvious major changes in my life at the time. My intuition was a little more pronounced and gradually increasing in availability and intensity.

I continued doing massage therapy and some energy healing on clients. After about eight or nine months, I realized that my massage clients were receiving energy healing without me attempting to do any healing work. It was emanating from me as appropriate. I began practicing more on my friends. I began doing more energy work as directed by my Guides.

All of my psychic senses were now open. I ended another relationship, and many friends had either exited my life or were also interested in spirituality or healing. This was a rather solitary time in my life when I spent most of my time focused on healing. I was having long discourses with my non-physical Guides, who taught me about many esoteric subjects. I was learning how to help people heal, the broader cycles of human life and the effects and necessity of personal empowerment.

Chapter Two

Light Language Arises

During a healing session, I would put the client on the massage table and utilize my original technique of gently moving my hands over their body while waiting for information of what was happening, or what was needed for the client in the moment. A few months after receiving an Axiatonal Alignment, I began to notice a twitching as I was doing energy healing, first in my stomach. Then my arm would twitch and my hand would move on its own. Other times I would be moving my hand and it would stop on its own. I was fascinated by this process, so I allowed my hands to move without my intention. Over the course of a few months, the movements got bigger and faster and I was soon doing a "hand dance" over my clients.

I loved the experience of my hands moving on their own above a client. It felt exciting and powerful, as if I had evidence that something extraordinary was happening to the client. I trusted energy healing implicitly by that point, because I had collected enough of my own experiences and those of my friends and family when I did healing work on them. But this was an interesting new development. Over the course of a few months, my hands began conducting an energetic orchestra in the energy field of my client. The energy felt smooth, loving, and powerful. I had to plant my feet strongly to accommodate the flow of the energy.

Because I was already clairaudient, I asked my Guides what was happening. I was accustomed to being taught what was healing or why. This time, I was told, "There are _____ number of people on Earth who do this." I don't remember the actual number, but it was under forty. This answer was completely unexpected. I had no frame of reference for it, because I didn't realize I was doing a different modality. I only knew that the experience of my hands moving on their own was different. When I asked, "Doing what? What am I doing?" my Guides would sometimes tell me what was healing for a client, but they would not elaborate beyond their original answer of the number of people who "do this."

I had never heard of Light Language nor been exposed to it in any way. I had vaguely heard of speaking in tongues, but I certainly had no idea you could sign in tongues!

Because I continued asking about the healing process, my Guides continued to answer in the way they felt was most beneficial for me. They would occasionally tell me the number of other people doing the same thing as me. Over the following months, that number went up and down. I did not understand that at the time, but years later it was validated that some people choose to shut it down. It was such a gentle opening for me, and I felt such curiosity and Love while it was occurring, that I felt no desire to stop it. My clients were responding well to it, even though I was just silently moving above them while their eyes were closed.

Based on this information from my Guides, I feel humanity was going through changes with Light Language in the early 2000s. My experiences with it began happening in early 2003. Because it stands to reason that the ability to speak in tongues was accessible to many more than forty-ish people worldwide, this information from my Guides indicated a difference in what was generally occurring for me and others. Light Language is speaking in tongues. However, a phenomenon that had once been associated exclusively with certain religions and shamanistic practices around the world, was now opening to another audience—like a natural gift being revealed in many individuals. New frequencies of information and healing became available to assist the current vibrational state of humanity. Even with the ups and downs of some people choosing to shut it down, the number has grown exponentially over the years and it still continues to increase.

Beginning in 2002 my Guides increased teaching me deep lessons on energy and healing as Light Language was opening within me, for it was only one part of my journey. They were establishing the

Crystalline Soul Healing® template[1], a separate energy healing modality that was being created through me. I didn't realize that was occurring at the time, I thought I was just following my natural inclinations of how to handle what I was learning. Even though I had two people spontaneously confirm that I was bringing through a healing modality, I felt too incapable of that. I pretty much just ignored it and kept following my passion of learning and healing. What arose as Crystalline Soul Healing® was a detailed program of healing that is a reflection of our Lyran cosmic heritage from my Guides. This way of working is aligned with our Ascension; for similar to Light Language, it is a communion with the human (physical) and higher (subtle) self becoming coherent and whole through deeper empowerment. It was a powerful journey of learning an advanced understanding of our energetic interaction and how to blend the laws of the subtle realm into the physical experience to support coherence within the self and others. It has been a profound journey of watching energy healers open to a deeper understanding of divine human capability.

    The learning phase of Light Language and Crystalline Soul Healing® congealing was fascinating and sometimes scary. But one step at a time, I was slowly building my courage and understanding. Through these years I also began to take some energy healing classes, which was helpful to speed my progress. Vianna Stibal's ThetaHealing® modality was particularly helpful, as it brought a connection with God/Source into the equation that I had been unconsciously resisting.

---

1   JamyePrice.com/what-is-crystalline-soul-healing

Light Language Grows

2005 brought great gifts and challenges as my intensified learning phase was strengthening to a new level. In February, a friend asked me to go to a healing workshop with her. I trusted her judgment that it was worth it. Boy, was it ever! At the workshop they projected pictures of written Light Language on a screen. As soon as I saw it, I knew my hands were writing Light Language in the air! It was a deep inner knowing—there was absolutely no doubt in my mind. I recognized the two-dimensional expression of what my hands were doing in the three-dimensional energy field of my clients.

Though this workshop was not about Light Language, the teacher spoke a transmission once. As I lay in bed that night, I wondered if I could also speak it and there it came! I let a little flow quietly aloud and some just inside my head. I asked to say, "I love you" in Light Language, and words flowed. It was a lovely experience, and I fell gently asleep. I still remember that Language clearly and I hear other people who speak it. While it is not one of my main Languages, I speak it occasionally as well.

Even letting Light Language flow aloud while I was alone tested my limits of courage and trust.

My opening to Light Language began in a small way and got bigger. What began as fascinating hand movements over a client whose eyes were closed became more challenging as the Light Language began to channel through my voice as well. When it was silently flowing through my hands over a client, I recognized a profound Love flowing through me that I was honored to allow. I just didn't feel comfortable with the sound or being that weird of a person! In order to keep the sound inside, I had to work hard during sessions to suppress it. But I was intent on suppressing it rather than letting it flow. Transmitting it alone was ultimately a lovely, though unusual, experience. Yet even letting Light Language flow aloud while I was alone tested my limits of courage and trust. Exposing that oddity to others was a risk I wasn't easily willing to take.

Channeling Light Language was so different from how I imagined my life would be, I felt like I would have to leave behind all that was normal to allow it. There was no information on the Internet when this began happening to me. YouTube was not available in the beginning, and for two years I didn't even know a term to search! I finally found Bryan de Flores's website in 2005—his and Reta Thomas Phillips's written Light Language had been shown at the workshop I went to earlier in the year. Yet after receiving clear validation of what I had been doing from Bryan's website, I instinctively knew I had to discover and choose my own path based on the direct experiences in my life.

In late 2005 I went to another workshop under odd circumstances. A new friend offered to pay my way into this workshop if I wanted to go, as I was offering her a place to stay while she attended it. I had the weekend free, so I went, though I knew little about the workshop except that the leader was a powerful woman from Singapore. This workshop was challenging because the teacher had severe ego issues. She was gifted, but she was also out of balance, so there were huge emotional blowups at unexpected times.

During this workshop, which was about thirty minutes from my home, I met my soul sister. We had similar experiences in the workshop, such as something that almost burst out of me (which I worked hard to suppress) burst out of my soul sister verbatim. Our bodies moved in comparable ways in response to the healing energy. A few days after the workshop, we decided to do some healing work together. It turned out we lived only a few blocks from each other in Los Angeles.

My soul sister's opening to Light Language was opposite of mine. She would go unconscious and her hand movements were huge. They got more specific and manageable over time and she began to be more conscious as she channeled Light Language. By the time we met, she was remaining conscious. Since we had distinct experiences, we were able to help each other find middle ground. She helped me have the courage to let it flow without holding it in. I helped her have the confidence to trust her intuition about what was happening.

I don't know if I would have had the courage to continue with Light Language if I hadn't met her. It was so peculiar with the movements and the sounds that I felt completely alone. It felt so loving and wonderful as it was happening, but dealing with the oddity by myself may have caused me to continue to repress it.

My soul sister and I worked together at least a few times a week for hours on end. We had many wonderful experiences that taught us so much. I heard Languages coming out of her that didn't come out of me, and vice versa. We validated information as we shared our experiences from the transmissions. Most importantly, my courage grew, as well as a grander connection to my Higher Self and the cosmos, which changed the course of my life.

Together with my soul sister, I discovered my limitations, my fears, and my misperception of them. The information that came through with the Light Language was fascinating. The experience of time, the collective experiences of humanity, even the blended nature of the soul were commonplace discoveries during this time. I watched as my body and voice played out energetic templates that we were working to heal—some personal and some collective. I learned so much about the nature of life through this form of communication I had kept hidden for years, simply because I feared judgment from others would overwhelm me.

We still work together as our journey of healing and growing continues. There will always be more to learn and improve in this lifetime. Healing is a wonderful journey of expansion, not a burden of imperfections that must be fixed.

At another workshop, also unrelated to Light Language, I met a man (who has chosen to remain anonymous) who wrote Light Language. His transmissions looked like squiggly lines, much different from anything I had seen before. However, I clearly felt the power of it, and to my surprise, I could also translate its meaning. The energy and depth of the transmissions was clear to me.

He has rare abilities. I have seen a lot of Light Language over the years, and his ability to insert such profound information and technology into his written transmissions is unique. A certain resonance of heart purity is required to access such innate technology. We worked together diligently, expanding our abilities rapidly. We had many experiences of validating information and intense energy upgrades. He moved out of the country for work so we no longer have the opportunity to work together as much, but our work was a valuable foundation for me regarding Light Language.

Taming the Fear

I was slowly growing the courage to let Light Language flow in private with like-minded friends. When I was around energy, such as during a beloved Kryon channeling (through Lee Carroll), my hands and body couldn't stay still unless I exerted a lot of effort. That is not a polite way to behave when others want to enjoy a meditative experience while listening to a channeling, so I relegated myself to the back of the room and worked hard to keep it manageable. It was difficult to hold it in. It felt like holding back a deluge of water that wanted to burst forth. I sat in the back of the room, shaking and twitching as silently as possible.

I would clamp my mouth shut as I sat on my hands. It was rather embarrassing. I wondered how my life had taken such a turn.

During this time, I found my soul brother. We were introduced at a spiritual event. As he was walking by, the person I was speaking with said, "I feel like you two should meet." The connection was immediate and profound, and another necessary support for me. We loved going to Kryon channelings (where you meet soul family!) and the Pineal Toning events of Dr. Todd Ovokaitys. My soul brother sat in the back with me as I twitched as quietly as possible. He made me feel safe and supported with his presence and acceptance of what I was experiencing.

It was more helpful than I can articulate to have someone who didn't also channel Light Language support me. It was like having a normal person accept my weirdness. I had already lost some dear friends that thought I was now too weird to be around. The only person who had seen it from the very beginning was my massage therapist, a beloved friend and intuitive test subject as I was learning. She lovingly told me once that she was happy to experience this with me in private, but she wouldn't want to be with me in public during it. I appreciated her honesty. It was valuable to have many types of support along my journey, even those friends I lost. With the support of loving people, I was beginning to have more courage to be myself.

I attended many Lee Carroll/Kryon events and finally decided to sit in the very back row and let the energy flow respectfully rather than just suppress it. I knew I could keep it as quiet as needed. I had friends on either side of me, so it was unlikely I would bother anyone. To my surprise, I found I didn't need to exert any effort to contain it. I could naturally allow it within the parameters of being respectful to everyone, including myself.

When necessary, it would whisper through me and my hands or body would move gently. At the time this was a bold move for me. If it got to be too much to contain, I got up and stood at the back of the room and let it move more fully, yet still quietly. That only ever happened during times that it was appropriately supported and wouldn't draw any attention from the presentation being given by the teacher.

A vendor in the back of the room saw me, and though she didn't know what I was doing, she felt so drawn to it that she asked me to do a session on her. This was a prompting from Spirit, assisting me to grow my confidence to share the Language of Light. I had never done a full-blown Light Language session on anyone other than a friend who was already familiar with it. It flowed just as easily, since I was open to allowing it.

The next year when I saw this woman at another event, I learned my session had activated Light Language within her. We worked together each year when she visited from Spain. She and my soul sister had never met, but I heard a Language come from both of them that never came from me. I was not aware of any examples of audible Light Language available online at the time. It was great validation for me that this is actual language that is accessed, not just random sounds. I didn't need proof by then, because I knew it to be true in my soul, but the human mind benefits from some evidence. This experience served to further support my nascent courage.

At that same event, I had a profound experience that validated something that had happened to me many years earlier. Lee Carroll was taking questions (as himself, not while channeling Kryon). A girl told him she had an experience where her hands started moving on their own and she spoke nonsense words. She went to a Peruvian shaman who told her she was possessed by the devil and he made it stop. She wanted to know what Lee Carroll thought about that.

My heart stopped.

I had no doubt that she had an experience like mine of channeling Light Language. I also had great respect and love for Lee Carroll's Kryon work—what would he say? Here I was, allowing it to flow quietly in the back of the room for the first time!

Lee Carroll told a story of going to a Pentecostal church once and observing from the back of the room. He said people stood up and spoke in tongues and it looked odd to him. There was an African woman visiting the church who approached a woman who had been speaking in tongues. Lee overheard her say that she was from a small tribe in Africa and that the woman had spoken her tribe's unique language and she understood every word! Because of that experience, Lee knew that speaking in tongues was authentic.

Lee then said to the girl at the event, "I believe that was God coming through you. The Peruvian shaman did what you wanted him to do, not because you were possessed by the devil, but because you wanted it to stop."

My heart started again! I received personal validation of what my Guides said early on as the number of people that "do this" went up and down. I also got indirect support from Lee Carroll. That event was a turning point for me. I had support from Life because I was beginning to honor myself instead of hiding.

Some time after the validation by Lee Carroll, I attended a workshop given by Todd Ovokaitys, MD. Known as "Dr. Todd," he offers Pineal Toning (sound healing for pineal gland activation) which I find extraordinarily beneficial. There was an evening celebration after the first night of the workshop. I was having fun dancing and talking to friends. I met a man named Kevin Gaspard and spoke to him briefly that evening. The next morning he brought me a Light Language transmission he had written for me, though we had never spoken about Light Language. So began another powerful friendship that continues to be a foundation of support and expansion on my journey of Light Language.

The next morning in the workshop, my right ear suddenly began popping uncomfortably. I later learned that Kevin was writing three powerful transmissions from across the room.

A little while later, three participants from the workshop walked the transmissions around to each table. As usual, I was sitting in the back of the room in order to keep my body movements unobtrusive. When the third transmission came around—BOOM! I went into channel. It was so powerful that it was hard to keep quiet, but I was doing my best. It was a profound experience. I was receiving an intense download and transmission of energy that was anchoring on Earth.

Though I was sitting in the back with my soul brother, our table was by the exit. My transmission lasted for about fifteen minutes. During that time, they decided to break for lunch, so most people ended up walking by our table to leave the room. Instead of leaving, some people stopped to watch me. Some were worried about me, because it looked so intense, while others were just curious about what was happening to me. My hands were flying around. I was crying at times, either as energy like sorrow released or as intense Love was anchoring. But to the outside eye it just looked like tears and uncontrollable movements.

As I was in channel, I heard bits of conversation; my soul brother was sitting there with me and quietly answered others' questions. I heard things like, "She's fine, she just anchors energy visibly." "No, it isn't harmful for her, though sometimes she may be tired afterwards." "It just started spontaneously when the last picture came around." I even heard him telling Kevin that his picture had started this.

All in all, it was a good experience. I had started a new friendship and working relationship with Kevin, who is able to bring through deep and powerful transmissions. I hadn't been able to hide the Light Language completely, and all was well. My courage was growing.

Final Steps Begin

I wasn't completely over the fear of being judged, though it no longer held me back as much because my passion for Light Language was stronger than my fear. I am grateful that my journey occurred as it did, for I grew my courage at the pace I could handle and support came in wonderful ways from friends I still love dearly. I was now honoring myself instead of suppressing myself. Well, mostly.

One day I sat down to meditate. I stated, "Okay, Universe, I want clear, clear, clear guidance of what you want me to do next!"

1. Be careful what you ask for.

2. Just because you say "clear" three times doesn't mean you're going to get every detail.

3. Do it anyway.

I did receive clear guidance. I was asked to channel Shiva (in English) at a specific location within a month. I agreed. Shiva would come in during Light Language transmissions at times, so I felt comfortable with his loving energy.

I had never channeled publicly before, only by myself. I had done automatic writing without knowing anything about it. I occasionally channeled in English during sessions, though I resisted it. But if channeling Shiva was my clear guidance from the Universe, I was going to follow it. My Aries nature helps me dive into new things with abandon.

I booked the location and oddly it was only available one Saturday that whole month. My event was about three and a half weeks away. I made flyers and distributed them. I practiced by channeling out loud into a recorder. I also practiced with some written channeling since I felt more comfortable with that format. I booked a healing session with someone and more "witch burning" past-life traumas released. Woohoo! I even got "sick" for about a week as intense energies were clearing from me in order to assist me in channeling more clearly.

A few days before the event, my Guides said distinctly, "Bring your [meditation] pillow because you're going to do darshan." I didn't know what "darshan" meant. I assumed it meant to hug someone, because I had heard that Ammachi, known as "The Hugging Saint," does darshan. My Guides showed me a specific hand gesture to do with one thumb on the third eye and two fingers on the occipital base. I was resistant, but I brought my pillow anyway. Of course, after the event I learned that "darshan" is a Sanskrit word meaning "transmission of light." What a beautiful synchronicity.

The day arrived and a super-excited friend and healer called me to wish me well. She was attending my event and had already thought about what she wanted to heal that night. She listed off about three big, broad issues. She doesn't do anything halfway!

The room was filled with about fifteen clients and friends. Just a lovely room of supportive people.

I assume the channeling went fine, since I have no recollection of it. Even though I am conscious while channeling, the memory of it doesn't last long. I wanted to record it, but mysteriously, I didn't press the right button on the recording device even though I used that recorder often. I am now clear that it was self-sabotage, which in cases of extreme fear is a survival mechanism. If I had that recording I would have listened to it and detested it, doubted it, and resisted channeling even more afterwards.

After the channeling I told everyone I was going to do individual healing work on them. They were to come up to the front and sit on the pillow one at a time. My super-excited friend was first, of course! She was ready to release! I remember seeing my finger slowly inching toward her. As I barely touched her, I moved fast and forcefully while screaming Light Language. What?! My Guides—no one in the Universe told me I was going to do that! They just showed me touching people on the forehead! I had asked for clear, clear, clear guidance!

I was mortified. The powerful burst of energy gave my friend a spontaneous kundalini awakening and she began laughing uncontrollably. She was not laughing at me, but I was still appalled at the embarrassing turn of events. The loud burst of noise also scared a young girl in the room and she started crying! It was my first time ever channeling Light Language in public, which I had to be tricked into doing, and I had made a child cry while my friend laughed hysterically. That's a fine how-do-ya-do!

I thought no one else would come up for me to do darshan on them after that, but everyone did. They were all supportive, and no one else inspired me to scream Light Language! We talked as a group after I finished doing darshan for everyone. I was able to hear what others had experienced as well as share information I had gotten during the transmissions. It was so helpful and encouraging. One client said she was glad it comes through me like a storm because she gets to see what is happening. Another client, the father of the young girl I made cry, booked a session for himself two days later.

> *My Guides had nurtured me into growing my courage through a timeframe that was appropriate for me, but now I was at a new choice point.*

During his session, I found myself holding back the Light Language sound again. I was hearing it in my head, but not letting it out of my mouth. At this point my Guides said to me very clearly, "It's alright. You can hold it in. It will just take him longer to heal." I knew exactly what they meant. It's not that Light Language is the only way or the best way to do healing work. All kinds of modalities are beneficial also. It was because I was holding myself back.

My Guides had nurtured me into growing my courage through a timeframe that was appropriate for me, but now I was at a new choice point. Here was someone wanting to heal—he had seen my Light Language at its loudest and it had even scared his own child to tears. Yet he still wanted to experience it. Now it was about me not allowing my natural way of healing to flow through.

I thought about that. Here is someone that just wants to heal. He was even paying me for my services. I could have done more for him, but I was too embarrassed or scared to be myself.

I just couldn't do that to someone. So I let it out.

I have never held it back since. I allow it as is appropriate, even though sometimes I'm only hearing it in my head because transmitting it out loud would be disruptive or uncomfortable to someone else. There is a vast difference between holding something back and honoring the environment. I am now courageous enough to do both.

Gentle Growth Continues

It took me six months to gather the courage to channel publicly again, either in English or in Light Language! I was allowing it to come through with clients since the experience after my first darshan, and by now I had been working with my Light Language friends for a while. My Guides asked me to channel again, so for three years I did a channeling in English and darshan in Light Language at my home once every two weeks.

Those bi-weekly channelings were helpful for building my courage, my abilities, and my understanding. I experienced different Languages coming through that were specific to a person or the group. I received validation about what I was transmitting. I was learning to recognize energies and various Languages. I was strengthening my resolve about not caring how weird it looked or if someone laughed—I understand how strange it looks and sounds, especially to someone who is not familiar with it. I was building endurance to transmit powerful energy for groups, as eventually my Guides said not to do individual work on people at my classes, though I still do individual private sessions.

Over the years, my clientele built by word of mouth. I was learning so much about Light Language. Crystalline Soul Healing®, the modality I developed separately from Light Language, was growing and running alongside my opening to Light Language.

When I work on clients, I run two complete modalities. Working with clients is a blessing to me, because I continue to learn through every person I meet. I enjoy getting to experience people while I am in a state of deep connection to Source Love and the universal communication of Light Language.

Throughout this time I was working a fulltime job at a corporation, as well as working on clients, teaching classes, and channeling every two weeks. My free time was spent doing work on myself or on others. I was singularly focused, and little else was happening in my life. I wasn't dating, and most of my friends were healers or at least open to it. I was able to completely immerse myself in my healing journey. Nothing meant as much to me.

The years of learning and growing courage were getting easier and even more interesting. The early years were a mix of fascination and fear, while the later years had the easier flow of less fear. My passion was so powerful that the fear had just slowed me down a bit.

Though there was one more time I almost had a change of heart.

My Guides told me I was to create healing audio with Light Language. That original message came to me around 2006. I knew nothing about making music, and I didn't have the money to fund the project. Luckily, I had a client who worked in the music industry. Everything I needed, this client had. I reached out to him about the project. Even though he loved my work, he wasn't available to help me.

I had no other avenues, so I put it on hold hoping I would eventually get to it. I felt guilty at times, as if I was just resisting, procrastinating or failing, but there wasn't a way I could have done it any sooner. Spirit often gives you a message before it is ripe. You will know it's ripe when things start to flow. Taking action is your part of the process. It will show you if it is appropriate to move forward. You don't let a "no" stop you, nor do you keep forcing things that aren't working. It's a fine line of balance.

About three years later, I got more detailed information about the project from my Guides. I still didn't know how I would do it, but I knew I was getting closer because the information was clearer. The following year I had a job change in corporate and was able to save the money to create the CDs, but I still didn't know how. I met new people who didn't end up being involved, but they led me to the person who was meant to help me.

I ended up at the studio of a wonderful Christian man. He was open-minded and supportive of my work. His loving energy was so helpful to me. He taught me about what he was doing as we were working. We recorded the Light Language, the guided meditations and the music separately. When I went home with the raw Light Language tracks (no music) and listened to them in my house by myself, I had a major emotional meltdown!

What was I doing?! This sounded crazy! Why did I leave corporate to do this?! I was miserable. I wanted to leave this crazy path behind. I sobbed and lamented for three days about what I had done to myself.

My emotions began to ease up as I just let the fear and pain release. With a new clarity, I realized I still had a passion for my calling to channel Light Language. I just needed to release the fear that was still within me. The Light Language tracks have a powerful energy to them. They release deeply, so just listening to them was bringing up a lot of pain. But once I got past that initial healing, I was fine and back on track.

By now I had been writing the Weekly LightBlast and Monthly Energies for many years in my newsletter. I had been including an audio Light Language transmission each month as well. I had gotten many requests to put it on video since the way I channel Light Language is so visual with all my movements. It took me months to gather the courage, but I finally did a monthly Light Language video for the newsletter. It was a much smoother process than my first public channeling!

After about a year or so of monthly video transmissions, a talk radio duo that likes to ridicule a channeler on each show evidently found my videos and chose to mock me. Suddenly I received a lot of mean comments on my videos. People were calling me insane and deluded, attacking my character and saying I'm what's wrong with the world, that I'm hurting people, and much more. Finally someone just wrote, "[The radio duo] sent me," and left me a smiley face. I was so grateful for that angel. I found out why I was suddenly getting such vicious comments.

The mean comments hurt me. I'm human—mean words hurt, nice words feel good. However, I was appreciative of the exercise. I had to work my way into courage and compassion, for myself and the commenters. I had to release any resentment toward the radio duo. It was clear to me they put others down to engage and increase their audience. I completely understand how weird Light Language looks and sounds to people who can't (or won't) allow themselves to feel the energy. I don't begrudge the commenters the right to their opinions. Even if they are expressing themselves with anger or in a negative way, that is not for me to take in. I'm responsible only for how I receive things.

> *"Am I in my integrity, even if someone else doesn't agree?"*

All in all, I was proud of how little it affected me. Though the comments didn't feel good, it eventually felt great to learn I was strong enough to experience a negative reaction to my beloved healing work and still continue to express myself. The benefits outweighed the negatives for me.

People still leave negative comments or judge me for things they don't agree with, whether it's Light Language or something else. Whenever it happens I do some inner searching. I ask myself things like, "Am I in my integrity, even if someone else doesn't agree?" "Am I being true to myself even if someone else doesn't like it?" If I feel I need to change something, I do. The choice to change must come from my inner promptings of what is right for me, not someone else. Mean comments or judgment will not stifle my heartfelt expression; rather, they are a gift of new courage and understanding.

Light Language Expands

Eventually my Guides told me I would teach Light Language to others, but it was not time yet. For two years they taught me about how to teach it to others. When I finally did the class, it was a weekend of tears of joy! I was amazed at the courage, determination, and abilities of each of my students. I was thrilled with the exercises my Guides had given me to help others open their capacity to channel Light Language.

Everyone in the class, whether complete beginner or not, was able to transmit Light Language, at least in one form (written, verbal, or signed) that felt good to them. They had a strong basis of understanding and tools to practice so they could continue to expand their abilities.

What deeply warmed my heart was they had community. The students met others who were interested in Light Language and were supportive of them. They forged relationships and felt accepted and included. They pushed past the same fears I had much more easily, because I am diligent about providing a supportive environment. They learned so much in one weekend. I was incredibly proud of each of them, which happens every time I teach this class. When I saw the effects of my Light Language class, I knew I had found a sweet spot. What a gift it was to be able to share something that would make others' journey easier than my own!

The morning after that first amazing Light Language class was complete, I had a serious headache, which was unusual for me. I also felt nauseous, which was so unusual that I couldn't even remember the last time I felt the sensation. I didn't know what was wrong, but it felt horrible—like a debilitating hangover without the party.

As I lay in bed feeling completely miserable, I got a short email from a student in the class. It was a wonderful email about how much she appreciated the class. I sobbed, much more than was warranted by the sweet email. With the spontaneous tears came a huge rush of energy that left my head. I had a brief flash of past-life fear and trauma releasing. I had to throw up immediately! After that I felt fatigued, but fine physically. All symptoms were gone. I've had some intense and interesting healing experiences, but none as immediate and visceral as that one.

When we take actions in life, they have an effect. By teaching that class, I was stepping into a fuller aspect of my path. Just by doing that I had a healing of unconscious fear and resistance. Living life to the fullest and sharing yourself is a powerful healing.

I hope to convey that through my fear and resistance I learned a lot, and through my courage, I gained a lot. Being an ambassador for Light Language is part of my soul path, which is why I felt compelled to share it, even through years of resistance. There was a deep love for Light Language within me, but I had to push past my fears to truly honor it, and to honor myself. The Language of Light was a catalyst for my self-discovery and it has opened me to life-altering knowledge and experiences. It has shown me what is truly important and how to be strong in the face of adversity, even though most of that adversity came from within!

My hope for you is that your interest in Light Language is a wonderful journey of discovery and connection, too. Perhaps yours will be easier and faster than mine. I hope you also find a bond with your Higher Self that illuminates your heart as mine has been. I pray you discover knowledge about the universal nature of Life as I have, and that you understand what a special part of it you are. Opening to Light Language has changed me forever and changed me for the better. I hope you find that, too.

Section Two

Light Language: Cohesive Humanity

What is Light Language?

This section begins with an overview of Light Language to assist your understanding of such a quantum and sacred communication. Then we examine its application into the subtle nature of life by relating it to frequency, light, geometry, and sound. Finally, we discuss the evolution of language and how this reflects a natural progression into conceptual and connective communication. This develops an understanding of what you are affecting—for yourself and humanity as a whole, as you allow the Language of Light into your life.

Chapter Three

Overview of Light Language

There are many answers to the questions about what the Language of Light is and what it does. Light Language is a broad concept and a varied experience. It is a richly layered form of communication within the subtle realms of existence. To understand it, one must comprehend some basic principles of the quantum nature of life, which this section will cover.

Underneath all of the information about Light Language, is a resonance of Love that is palpable to the many people who are open to it. It often inspires tears, a knowing, or a longing for "home." This response is an unconscious recognition of the Languages and an indication of healing. It is an experience of great release and shift in emotions as one interacts with the vibrational frequency of Love—the connective language of the heart. Much of the clarity of Light Language is within the trust of the unknown; this trust heals through mental barriers by dissolving heart barriers.

The Language of Light in its purest sense is information. Like the vacuum of space, it contains deep instructional information that builds form. It can be written, spoken, sung or signed as it moves through your voice, hands and body. This Language, the information, is transmitted via Light. The information is much more than what is visible or audible; *it is the information of loving intent and connection,* and thus it is deeply layered. It is composed of audible and inaudible instructions that shift your vibration and improve your experience. It is a pure transmission of Love, which is a higher-frequency (less dense) communication than just words.

Much of the clarity of Light Language is within the trust of the unknown; this trust heals mental barriers by dissolving heart barriers.

Light Language is like a library condensed into sound, symbol and/or movement. It is actual language that is being transmitted, but it is not typically as linear as human languages. It is a multidimensional communication form with many layers of information that your biomechanism can utilize for healing and learning. It can be transmitted and received through direct telepathic transference, without hearing or seeing it. In short it can operate at levels beyond your conscious mind, though *it is always your Higher Self utilizing the encodements*, the information, as appropriate for each moment.

Multidimensional Language

Light Language is *dynamic* sound and light encodements that interact with your energy field. It triggers a change response that balances your vibrational information in the moment. Your Higher Self initiates your unique response to the transmission.

You receive, understand, and utilize the quantum information of the Language of Light on an unconscious level for your physical, emotional, mental, and spiritual healing. Each time you interact with a transmission, your energy field is different, so it affects you differently according to your current needs.

For example, as you listen to the recording of my Sacred Relationship Light Language audio, you may first release vibrational data of trauma from losing loved ones throughout your past, even in other lifetimes. Your vibration is now changed and will balance into a calmer state of being at peace with loss. The Light Language has helped you unconsciously (or consciously) grieve and resolve pain. The next listening may release fear of judgment or abandonment. Another listening will download a cellular understanding of deep intimacy and compassion without manipulation or codependency. You are not consciously directing the healing, nor am I. I allowed the transmission through, and your Higher Self initiates any change (a release and activation of information) that is for your highest good. Interacting with multidimensional Light Language can inspire endless variables of experience.

Your Higher Self initiates your unique response to the Light Language transmission.

There are many variations of Light Language. Some Languages have more of an angelic basis and focus mainly on physical or emotional healing. Many people notice a strong emotional reaction to angelic Language, like tears or a feeling of deep love.

Other Languages are predominantly elemental, like elven or faerie. These Languages align humans with nature and many fields of science. Often a listener will report a feeling of joy or connection to nature during an elemental transmission.

Some Light Language is galactic in origin and helps to elevate mental and technological information that assists humans to increase healthy evolution. Galactic Light Language can originate from many different races, and even different time streams from the same galactic races.

In some transmissions, there is an earthly origin to the Languages. These Languages are often the most easily recognized because we have such a conscious and physical connection through our DNA. This may be xenoglossia, where the channel accesses a Language that is known on Earth, though unknown to the channeler. It may be glossolalia as a past or future time stream of the Earth experience is accessed.

The Language of Light is generally not translated word for word. *It is a deeply layered alchemical transmission of information.* It frequently sounds and looks like various Earth languages. Listeners may identify it as sounding Aramaic, Native American, Asian, or another human language. In written form it may look like an offshoot of Arabic, Sumerian cuneiform, or Sanskrit, to name a few. Conversely, it may not look like any Earth languages.

During a group transmission, one person might think the dialect sounds Persian, while another hears an eastern European dialect, for example. Each person is correct. The frequencies are adjusted through each person's Higher Self for his or her best healing potential in the moment. Each person hears and perceives through the filter of his or her own energy resonance.

Light Language is not bound by linear time. Each transmission can be a unique blend of Languages from various time streams and energy resonances. It may include aspects of ancient human languages and future human languages. It may be a transmission from non-human energies, such as angels, elementals, certain animal species or various galactic races.

Though I channel many different Languages of Light, I commonly channel Sirian, ancient Egyptian or Lyran/Pleiadian Language. I had a unique experience while publicly channeling Areon, which is the Lyran Council of Time, in English. Toward the end of the channeling, Areon said, "We are now going to speak to you in our original language." That particular

Language was not something I had channeled before, and because my frequency was not accustomed to it, it was slightly challenging to channel. The difference in the time stream was palpable and audible to me, as well as to those in the room who were familiar with the Light Language during those channelings.

Why Now?

Light Language is merely a unique form of channeling. Since every human is a biomechanism that is constantly receiving and emitting frequencies, it is simply a matter of attuning yourself to consciously receive and emit the unique frequencies of the Language of Light. One's vibrational foundation of Love creates a resonance with the basis of creation—Love. As we move through Ascension, we are aligning with the natural capability of multidimensional communication.

Light Language is not new to Earth. Its origin is known as "speaking in tongues" to some religions and also various terms from shamanistic practices throughout the world. There are references to it in many ancient texts, including the Bible. The technical terms for these abilities are glossolalia, speaking languages of unknown origin; and xenoglossia speaking a language unknown to the speaker, but common to other humans—as in the example Lee Carroll heard at the Pentecostal church.

During the Pentecost, Jesus descended unto his disciples in a flame, hence the flame depicted above the head of the Pentecosts. This represents the merging of the Ascended Jesus with humans dedicated to a path of elevation. This merging raises their frequency and they exhibit gifts of healing or "tongues" after the experience. In Hinduism, this relates to shaktipat, where a transfer of energy with an enlightened being can assist an aspirant through a transformative kundalini experience.

Based on my channeled information, there are frequencies of Light Language now consciously available that were not previously viable for assisting humanity. There is a new accessibility, variety, intensity, and interest in it. It is ultimately the same thing as speaking in tongues, but with an expanded nomenclature that reflects a blend of quantum science and spirituality.

Light Language is varied because each human carries a unique signature of angelic, galactic, elemental, and ancestral energies—a unique cosmic heritage. This broad availability of many types of cosmic Languages is perhaps the greatest difference between the Language of Light and speaking in tongues. Comparing Light Language and speaking in tongues is the equivalent of comparing modern dance to ballet. Modern dance has its origins in ballet; some of it is similar in appearance, while some of it appears quite different, yet both are dance.

> **Light Language is an expression of the higher-frequency information of Love.**

The Language of Light is coming forth increasingly at this time because it is a powerful catalyst for the Ascension of humanity—our natural evolution into a higher frequency, a higher resonance of Love. We are beginning to open to additional aspects of our innate divine nature as our frequency raises. As humanity evolves into a deeper awareness of the connected nature of all of Life, it begins to open to communication that enhances this connection and understanding. As your personal vibrational frequency calibrates faster (higher), you are more consciously aware of higher-frequency information—Love. *Light Language is an expression of the higher-frequency information of Love.*

The Nature of the Unknown

The Language of Light has an inherent quality of allowing. It requires that each individual move from trying to control the outer world to honoring the inner world. This is the first step in creating a better life and an important lesson humanity as a whole is learning.

Your inner world comprises your mental and emotional aspects. It can easily feel as if you have no control over your inner experience as the world pushes and pulls at you with drama, obligation and fear. If the outer world is controlling your inner world consistently, there is an imbalance within you that is inhibiting your feeling of empowerment and sovereignty over your inner domain. Light Language helps to heal aspects of the self that often aren't even recognized as closed until the gates of empowerment and connection open. As you interact with the Language of Light, you engage your quantum nature in a form of conscious sound and light interplay that helps you understand that Life is supporting you beyond what you may have perceived.

As a disempowered human, you operate without awareness of your inner signals. As an empowered human, you do not just blindly trust; you discern with your innate senses and choose what feels appropriate for you. Your intuitive senses naturally read tone of voice, body language, give you "goosebumps," or a "gut feeling" and have many ways of alerting you to whether experiences are positive or negative for you. It merely requires listening to your inner signals.

With Light Language, the discernment first comes as a feeling of, "This is or is not right for me based on what my heart feels, not what my brain thinks." It is a powerful aspect of discerning new information rather than echoing reiterations of the previously known. This discerning is based on what is unknown to your intellect, but known in your heart. That is a beautiful paradox.

As humanity evolves into a deeper awareness of the connected nature of all of Life, it begins to open to communication that enhances this connection and understanding.

Paradox occurs when your mind meets two opposites that may each be true. In the case of Light Language, the paradox is, "I know and I don't know." As you open to paradox, you expand beyond a previously defined right or wrong and into a deeper understanding of the dual nature of life. The Language of Light and paradox help you understand with your infinite heart rather than just with your mind. Paradox is a tipping point of expansion as your truth encompasses more wisdom about life. This brings you into greater coherence as a whole being, combining mental and emotional intelligence.

Do No Harm

Humanity is endowed with free will. Free will is your internal choice of what you will accept into the sovereign aspect of self, which is composed of your mental and emotional aspects. For example, you do not choose what goes on around you, such as a stranger on the street saying something derogatory to you. However, you do have the ability to choose how you let the stranger's words affect your mental and emotional vibration.

Light Language is a pure transmission of Love that will do no harm. Because humanity does not understand the Languages, it cannot bypass free will. Because there cannot be conscious agreement, there cannot be deception. True Light Language cannot manipulate the person who is receiving it because it is a divine tool of creation. *Your Higher Self is the vehicle of choice and functionality for the transmission.*

Each human who transmits or receives Light Language has their human ego filters of perception and desire upon the transmission. Inherent in transmitting Light Language is an ability to rise above the filters to a certain extent, but not completely. An imbalanced human ego can flavor the information. In other words, the Light Language is pure, while the human channel may not be. A person receiving a transmission may respond to the ego intent of the human transmitting, even though the Language of Light is always purely loving.

For example, a human channel may have a need for devotion and admiration from others, stemming from an imbalanced ego that nurtures low self-esteem through attention from others. This imbalance would not necessarily be obvious to most people; no one announces they have an ego imbalance, they merely behave in unconscious ways to satisfy it. One listener may receive transmissions from this channeler and go about life normally, even benefitting greatly from the channel's work. Another listener may find he or she is thinking about the channeler constantly, feeling a need to be with the channeler, and devoting time to support him or her in any way possible. It may elevate to the point of obsession, denigrating others, poor financial decisions and separating from family or friends.

Light Language itself is a communication of higher-frequency Love that has no resonance with overpowering others. The listener who responds detrimentally to the ego intent of the channeler has a resonance with low self-esteem that manifests in a congruent way with the channeler—both need attention. One is seeking to be master—holding power over another. One needs to be a devotee—giving power to another.

I have observed this in a group setting as a human channel's energy field was working contrary to the Light Language they were transmitting. Those in the group with no resonant ego imbalance were impervious to the channeler's egoic needs. The Light Language has the potential to keep working with the channeler to heal the ego imbalance, but the human must make the choice to change. This is often not a smooth process, because humans with imbalanced egos are resistant to changing.

As you interact with a Light Language transmission, discern with detached observation (no strong mental or emotional bias) what you feel and sense. If you feel it to be inharmonious with you, honor that, for that particular experience isn't for you. Perhaps your vibration is more suited for a different frequency. For example, humans with a deep angelic resonance may not feel as drawn to a galactic transmission. If your heart pulls toward it, engage. Release the binds of your resistance to the unknown and Know you are expanding appropriately. Trust yourself. Use your wise discernment of what does or does not feel right for you.

__Light Language conveys a wonderful synergy of enhancing your vibrational state through the power of Love.__

Your Higher Self filters the Light Language encodements for your best advantage. You receive the energies that are aligned with your intent. Your intent is the totality of information behind any thoughts, words, or deeds, as the aforementioned example demonstrated. If your intent is not empowered enough to benefit from the frequencies, your Higher Self may naturally direct you away from that transmission.

Your empowered intent—knowing you are protected and healing or expanding from a place of self-love—filters through any egoic disruptions from a person transmitting Light Language. Your disempowered intent—feeling inferior or desperate for example—may bring beneficial lessons to help you strengthen your empowerment. The lessons will call you to more empowered interaction. Light Language conveys a wonderful synergy of enhancing your vibrational state through the power of Love.

Profound Change

Part of the beauty of Light Language is that it unfolds through *you* because your logical mind cannot attribute it to someone else. You cannot deconstruct the information as you would with something you logically understand. Therefore, it has a greater potential to bypass the mental limitations you may have. *Light Language speaks the connective language of the heart rather than the known language of the mind.*

It is possible to undo the maximal benefit of energy healing in different ways. One may doubt or overlook the subtle clues of healing and new choices in their life. Another may continue the same thought patterns, emotional responses, and physical actions that previously imbalanced the ability to adapt and create life with greater ease.

As the Language of Light interacts with your energy field, it behaves like a time-release capsule. It unfolds healing in an invisible sequence through time as your Higher Self cascades the opportunities for your best growth and change. While it is possible to negate the healing effects of Light Language as noted above, it offers a profound opportunity for your Higher Self to guide your improvement.

Light Language speaks the connective language of the heart rather than the known language of the mind.

Change is generally not huge in any given moment. It grows just like a seed does: bit by bit, moment by moment, and each small change is appropriate for the season of growth or situation. Are you in a time of rooting yourself deeper for foundational support and change? If so, your changes won't be as visible to you, but they will be profound when they come into your awareness, and often will not be directly attributable to a past healing experience. Are you in a time of expansion and blossoming? Then rejoice in the scent-ual experience and appreciate all the invisible rooting that took place to support this blooming. As you release resistance to your season of growth, you allow yourself to access the full potential Light Language offers you, thereby enhancing its effect.

SACRED COMMUNICATION

One of the myriad reasons this modality is called Light *Language* is that communication is at its core. However, the informational aspect has less to do with the "words" being transmitted, than with the depth of change and connection being offered through the multilayered vibrational communication of vast creational information.

The power of Light Language is an intense reminder of a deeper communion with Life. Communion is a sacred sharing, and it is the basis of the Language of Light. Humanity is strengthening into a greater level of connection with All Life. As you receive a transmission from another or allow it to flow directly through you, you open your physical vehicle to a communion with your Higher Self and the core of Love. This is your true nature. You are initiating an anchoring of sacred communion here on Earth. Your cells change, your perceptions change, and thus your future changes. This ripples out to affect others, the Earth, and our multiverse in ways that are currently incalculable.

The Language of Light is a fascinating discovery of human capability. *The ability to communicate in a more conceptual and connected way is a profound advancement for humanity.* It is an esoteric experience that is not easily defined—there is no complete dictionary for it. As we uncover what Light Language means to humanity, we begin to discover a heritage beyond our physical birth. We recognize a continual unseen connection to other realms of existence that are ultimately not so separate from humanity. We begin to honor our inevitable Ascension, the natural evolution into our inherent divine nature. The emergence of Light Language is an indicator of humanity's growth into fourth density physicality, which occurs in spurts before it becomes the new norm. Light Language creates greater communication and connection, both with one another and the subtle realms. The journey of life expands.

Chapter Four

Energy, Frequency, and Vibration

"If you want to find the secrets of the universe, think in terms of energy, frequency, and vibration."
—Nikola Tesla

At the core of all physical matter is pure energy. As scientists study small particles, they discover that subatomic physical structures are composed of wave properties. Energy, frequency, or vibration is the formless, the subtle, or the invisible to human senses. What brings energy into form is the great mystery of science. Quantum physicists include the role of the observer as effecting waveform properties into particle form. Esoterically this observance is known as consciousness, awareness, focus, or Love. Your life is the potential of energy in which you reside. Your attention and focus shapes it into form.

The famous Double Slit experiment[1] exemplifies that extremely small particles, like photons or electrons, exhibit both particle and wave properties, and those properties can be affected by observation. In the experiment, scientists recorded the behavior of single electrons being passed through two slits and discovered the single electron behaved like a wave. It created an interference pattern (a wave property) on the wall, rather than the two single lines that would be expected from matter.

They decided to record data earlier in the process. To determine which slit each electron went through, they added a measuring device directly at the start of the slits rather than the final destination of the wall. To their surprise, the electron began behaving like a particle rather than a wave. This same experiment was repeated with light (photons), and the results were the same. By adding a simple observation mechanism (the measuring device) directly at the electron or photon, the behavior of the particle changed from exhibiting waveform properties to demonstrating the behavior of physical matter.

This phenomenon is now known as the Observer Effect. Even something minutely small being viewed by an observer, is affected by the act of observation. Because of the Observer Effect, the mere act of an observer interacting with an electron changes

---

1   http://physics.about.com/od/lightoptics/a/doubleslit.htm

its wave-like behavior into particle-like behavior. When it is not being directly observed, it behaves like a wave.

> *Theoretically the Light Language transmission is in wave form, and the observer collapses the wave into particle form as the Language of Light interacts with their energy field. Intent shapes the wave.*

My experience is that Light Language also reflects the Observer Effect; theoretically the transmission is in wave form, and the observer (the one receiving a transmission) collapses the wave into particle form as the Language of Light interacts with the receiver's energy field, their density of information. Intent shapes the wave. The Higher Self of each being determines what will release and/or activate during each transmission by receiving the vast encodements (waveform properties) and choosing specific results (particle properties).

FREQUENCY

Energy, whether in particle or wave form, causes the field around it to vibrate. The wave frequency determines the rate of vibration. Higher-frequency waves cause matter to have a less dense physical structure (for example, aerogels or aerographene), or a higher-pitched sound in the case of sound waves. Lower-frequency waves cause matter to have a denser physical structure (such as mercury or basalt), or a lower-pitched sound. Within a spectrum accessible to your physical senses, you see this as light and hear it as sound; you also taste, touch, or smell it. Your senses convert frequency data into the experience of sight, taste, touch, smell, or sound.

Light Language helps entrain your vibration to a higher vibration of Love and health.

Your physical structure has a mix of frequencies within it, just as the earth does. Your liver vibrates at a different frequency than your intestines. Your vibration is in a constant state of flux. Your emotions and thoughts also have a vibration to them. They are not dense enough to have a solid form, yet they both affect your solid form and cause chemical reactions in your body. For example, a thought of anger causes a hormonal release. This automatically stimulates certain physical reactions to occur, like faster breathing and reduced digestion. Thus the vibration of your thoughts and emotions is quite influential, especially to your physical health and the physical realm in general.

In the 1980s, Rene Peoc'h did extensive research about the phenomenon of thoughts influencing physical matter. In one famous experiment, he put newly hatched chicks in one cage, and a robot that moved around in the next cage with a random event generator (REG). The chicks imprinted on the robot as if it were their mother, which is a natural behavior for chicks. As the robot randomly moved farther away from them, they desired it to be near.

The overall result of many different tests was that the chicks were able to influence the robot to be closer to them well beyond statistical probability. In other words, the chicks influenced the REG computer program with their desire for the robot (who they perceived as a mother) to be closer to them.

Resonance

Waves entrain to their environment. This principle is based on resonance, the phenomenon of waves interacting due to energy being transferred between them. It was first noted in 1666 by physicist Christiaan Huygens, who observed the synchronization of the pendula on multiple clocks.

A lower-frequency wave will generally increase its frequency toward a higher one, although the higher-frequency wave does slow to match a lower frequency as well.

The observation of resonance can also apply to your life. For example, a nursing mother's physical body responds to a crying baby and produces milk. She resonates—she experiences a change in her own vibration due to the sound waves the crying baby makes. She becomes compatible with the crying baby and produces the food it needs.

When you experience resonance with someone or something, your vibrations are compatible. You may also sense a discordant vibration easily. When you encounter a vibration that is much higher or lower than your own, you sense the discord—though often one feels better than the other.

The Language of Light creates a resonant effect with your vibration. Much more than mere sound or shape, it is the multilayered informational frequency of the harmony of Love because it is a foundational creation-language flow. Light Language helps entrain your vibrational setpoint to a higher resonance of Love and health. It helps you release emotional, mental and physical distortions that are lowering your vibration.

My own countless experiences with the healing effects of Light Language have compelled me to share it with others. I have observed many other people experience healing effects from it as well. While this experiential data is anecdotal evidence, indeed it is the basis upon which all exploration begins.

The Power of Perception

Humanity knows everything has a vibration. The flowers you can see, smell, touch, taste and now hear (with special equipment), are pure vibration. Molecules create the structure you observe, and your senses interpret their vibration. In essence, you are sensing the vibration between the bonds of the molecules; you are sensing the boundary conditions that create visible or other sensual form. When you can smell, taste, touch,

Energy, Frequency, and Vibration | 69

hear, or see something, you call it real. It seems solid, and indeed it is in this reality—but there is more to it than the solid form you experience.

> ***You are not only sensing through a range of frequencies, you are discerning through your emotional and mental perceptions as well.***

You logically understand that a kitchen table is comprised of a mass of molecules made up of subatomic particles that are constantly vibrating. Yet your senses interpret the dense/low frequency of the table as solid. The inductive reasoning (which begins as, "I see and feel a solid table") of the solidity of the table transfers to the solidity of life.

As a practical example, this kind of reasoning naturally leads you to think the behavior of your ornery boss is solid and unchangeable, and that your own perception and mental focus have no bearing upon it. The hard fact of the table leads to the idea of the hard fact of the boss's behavior. The frequency of your thoughts and feelings are not deemed as having any impact on the situation, because indeed, they have no discernable effect on the table.

Physical perceptions are intermingled with emotional perceptions as well. You may say an item is green, but green is an individual perception. To you the item may be vibrant and joyful, but to someone else it may be ugly and seem dull, though both are looking at the same item. *You are not only sensing through a range of frequencies, you are discerning through your emotional and mental perceptions as well.* For instance, your boss's behavior may have upset you, but another co-worker may feel the boss's behavior was perfectly reasonable.

To summarize, there is a range of frequencies that your human senses define into smell, sound, taste, touch, and sight; and there is a range beyond that which you cannot physically discern—such as ultra-violet or infra-red light. You are surrounded by and you interact with all of these frequencies, though many are imperceptible to your physical senses. The range of frequencies that humanity interacts with is subject to personal interpretation that is so natural, many don't realize they are having a unique experience. All that you interact with, whether consciously or unconsciously, is affected by your vibration, your perception, and your observation.

This discussion of energy, frequency, and vibration is meant to help you understand the invisible aspects of Light Language on a deeper level. The Language of Light, as any experience, is pure energy vibrating at a rate that converts information into a manifestation of sound and light. This manifestation is intermingled with an emotional, mental, and physical experience. It also has a frequency range beyond human sensory perception. This is why so many react with tears, a feeling of knowing, or a heartfelt connection.

The Language of Light contains the frequencies of creational information that stimulate your ability to feel Divine Love; it informs and entrains your vibration to a higher frequency of Love. It changes your frequency with each interaction. Your intent to improve, however, is the most powerful stimulus when combined with the Language of Light.

Light Language helps your vibration ascend into mastery of the human form. You begin to choose your life experiences rather than just allow outside circumstances to dictate your vibrational state. Jesus spoke of this as being the peace that passes all understanding. Masters such as Jesus, Buddha, and many others have exemplified a high vibrational state in human form. They displayed gifts of healing, intuition, and wisdom that easily flowed from them. This is actually a natural part of humanity's ascended state into a higher vibration of Love. It is the reason Jesus said (paraphrased), "All that I do, you shall do, and more." (John 14:12) Are you ready to do more? Light Language is one gift humanity accesses as we each improve and increase our individual energy, frequency, and vibration. The Language of Light entrains you to a higher vibration, your higher vibration of Love ripples out into the world, and life on Earth changes.

Chapter Five

The Quantum Nature of Light

Science is working to corroborate the quantum nature of light and life. In the Double Slit experiment, it was exhibited that light has both wave and particle properties, a dual behavior that has finally been captured on film.[1] The Observer Effect theorizes that the observer influences the outcome of reality, or the resulting form and behavior of light. Without an observer, the light behaves as a wave. When an observer is present, the wave collapses into particle. I observe this same phenomenon with Light Language.

---

1   http://actu.epfl.ch/news/the-first-ever-photograph-of-light-as-both-a-parti/

Wave or Particle Light

When I began doing group transmissions, which was after much practice working on individuals, I noticed with my intuitive senses that the energy was working in different ways on the individuals in the room. As my Guides explain it, the Higher Self of each individual activates the Light Language encodements as needed. The transmission is delivered as both wave and particle form, as exemplified in the picture referenced previously. *The broader consciousness of an individual collapses the wave properties into particle properties which directly and specifically affects his or her physical, mental, emotional, and spiritual nature.*

The wave property of light is highly malleable. It is not subject to the laws of Newtonian physics. It is entangled beyond time and space, and therefore able to effect change without those limitations. It is not limited to human understanding; rather it is undefined enough to be open to a vast array of possibilities. It may have a resonance of variability (a structure of a general nature), but the wave functionality opens it to the needs of the observer, who then shapes or magnetizes the waves into particle form.

The kitchen table is subject to Newtonian physics; most humans are currently unable to affect the table's properties with thought alone. It is a densely bonded particle-form structure, even though, at its core, it is made up of vibrating subatomic particles. The dense frequency of the table is not malleable to thought-form frequency. You cannot think a table into a new shape or color. However, the less dense frequency of the Language of Light is malleable to the Higher Self of a person receiving a transmission.

For instance, a Light Language transmission about abundance heals layers of physical, emotional, mental, or spiritual blockages that will be activated as needed by the receiver. In a group, perhaps one person may have emotional blockages with regards to feeling worthy, while another may begin to release the physical causality of a disease or an unconscious past-life trauma. Perhaps another person finds forgiveness for a boss in their first listening. In the next listening that same person heals some layers of a challenging relationship with a deceased parent. Many layers of healing happen at once, though not all of the information is known. Sometimes healing occurs in stages based on a need for deeper understanding, conscious choice to change, ease of transition, or even resistance to change.

HOLOGRAPHIC REALITY

I believe we live in a holographic reality. I recommend reading *The Holographic Universe* by Michael Talbot for a more in-depth study of this topic. The holographic nature of life supports the physical reality and the nonphysical reality of life. It is deeply embedded with the functionality of light.

A hologram is the appearance of a three-dimensional (length, width, depth) picture from a flat surface. It is created by a single beam of laser light that is split. Part of the split beam is reflected off of the object being rendered into holographic form. The other part of the beam is reflected onto the film. As these two beams intersect, they create an interference pattern that is recorded onto the film and forms a holographic picture.

Your awareness collapses and shapes the wave into particle, while your perspective influences the particle form.

If a holographic picture is cut in half or even more, the entire three-dimensional picture is still available within the pieces. Here you begin to understand the connection between the fractal and holographic nature of life. The whole is contained within the parts, and there is always another layer in both directions (larger or smaller). There cannot be a part without a whole. This is the fractal nature of life. Mind-boggling and mind-opening at the same time.

Light is a carrier vehicle of information. It is vast and multilayered. It contains the information of the whole and the smaller part(s). Your light is your consciousness. Your (holographic) reality is created by your specific reflection of light/consciousness. It is your unique *perception* (how you take in information) and your unique *perspective* (your views and beliefs that you have established). Your perception is your receiving of life, and your perspective emanates out of you as vibration. Life on Earth is your observed reality, and your consciousness affects your reality. Your light is your unique perspective illuminating your experiences and the world around you.

Your consciousness and your unique perspective act as a holographic apparatus that creates reality. *Just as a hologram is created by the unique reflection of a single beam of light, your unique perspective creates your reality.* As you shift your perspective, you shift your reality. Your awareness collapses and shapes the wave into particle, while your perspective influences the particle form. Your choice is a vehicle of change as you shift your perceptions and perspectives, affecting your experience of life and the frequency that is building form in the future. This exemplifies the quantum nature of light and your unique perspective—your beam of light, creating your (holographic) reality.

The Language of Light helps you find your own quantum nature, indelibly connected to All Life.

Light Language reflects this holographic and fractal nature and helps you shift your perceptions and perspectives. The wholeness of its expression is the vast malleable waveform, awaiting your unique perspective to illuminate the fractal parts contained within. Light itself is as open and unconditional as Love. It responds to your perspective with a detachment that would give up its freedom of wave form to bind into particle for you, even if you were experiencing a moment of hatred or rage. The Language of Light has this same impartiality to your choice as it envelopes you in a wave of Love and awaits your awareness to bind it into particle form. This awareness generally occurs on an unconscious level first. Your Higher Self, your innate wisdom, is the filter and overseer of this path—lovingly assisting you to improve your life.

In *The Keys of Enoch* (Hurtak, 1999) Light Language is referenced as "Instant communication with the Infinite Mind" indicating a vibrational resonance with a vast interworking of the creative force. Your biomechanism is naturally prepared for the evolution of Light Language. It is merely the season of growth and your inner adjustment that opens you to it. The Language of Light helps you find your own quantum nature, indelibly connected to All Life and yet unique, loving, and powerful. Light Language is a wave of Love in verbal, written, or signed form. You make it particle form.

Chapter Six

Sacred Geometry

Early on, when I began to understand that Light Language was transmitting through me, I asked my Guides to tell me more about it. Archangel Metatron came forth and said:

> The frequency of the Light Language creates the *geometries* that are needed spatially in the person's Lightbody. Like a solar flare, it is a powerful burst that bypasses all other encodements or transductions because it immediately hits the energy field without having to be broken down into other formats, like an understanding or an emotion. It immediately interacts with the Lightbody.

Geometry is a fascinating study of angles that create shapes. Geometry can be understood as mathematical formula, music, or relationship. An angle creates a relationship, and the overall shape is dependent upon multiple angles, both seen and unseen. The angles determine the strength, and even the boundary conditions, of the shape. This is the basis of the phi ratio, or the golden mean ratio, which explains how nature creates the strongest form. The Fibonacci spiral is more than a beautiful shape or basic math. It is a key to the formulation of life, including your physical body, as Leonardo da Vinci demonstrated in his drawing, *Vitruvian Man*. It holds the secrets to the relationships that create the shapes of Life. It demonstrates that life builds upon itself.

> ***Geometry can be understood as mathematical formula, music, or relationship.***

Astrology is the study of how the angles of the planets affect reality. The location of the planets to you, and also to other planets, create an overall shape of energy. For instance, when planets are at a ninety-degree angle to each other, this "square" of planets represents a more challenging aspect of energy. Nature does not often create ninety-degree angles, as it is not the strongest angle available—it is easily collapsed. That is good news in relation to the challenges of your life, as the astrological squaring angle of opposition is easily collapsed. Ultimately, your challenges are, too.

MASCULINE ENERGY AND FEMININE ENERGY

Straight lines represent masculine energy, which is direct, active, and electric. Curved lines represent feminine energy, which is circuitous, receptive, passive, and magnetic. Just like the merging of the masculine and feminine that is required to create new human life, these opposite energies are two sides of one coin. For example, upon observing a sphere, only the curved feminine lines are visible. However, within that sphere is an incredibly strong vacuum, known as the vector equilibrium, which is composed of the strongest angles (masculine lines) that nature creates.

> *Your choice is the powerful magnetic bonder within you.*

This vector equilibrium within the sphere, brought forth by Buckminster Fuller, has been detailed into a profound yet easily understood format by Nassim Haramein. A deeper study of his work is highly recommended.[1] Haramein discovered the secret to the Tree of Life as creating this vector equilibrium (esoterically, when the feminine, the reflection, is

---

1   http://resonance.is/

honored), as well as the I Ching creating that same structure. The numerology and geometry within these two ancient systems are equally profound. The vector equilibrium, which is the glue that shapes a sphere, is represented by the Flower of Life, as it creates that shape in two dimensions.

Geometry is a physical representation of the power of magnetics—that lines and angles are the masculine nature of life bound through the feminine nature of life, and vice versa. This constantly moving interplay creates form. This movement and interplay is represented in the yin/yang symbol, which further represents the toroidal shape that is created by the spiraling within. Without the invisible magnetic force the spiraling creates, form is unable to bond. Your choice is the powerful magnetic bonder within you. Word is a direction of energy, a line awaiting form. Observe the lines and curves in your own life: your words, actions, relationships, career, and more. The clues of creation are revealed.

> ***Geometry is a physical representation of the power of magnetics.***

To further encapsulate your understanding, below is a channeling I received about sacred geometry from Melchizadek, an ascended master. It relates how your choice affects geometries—the shape of your life.

To understand sacred geometry, one can begin simply, with high math, or with intricate music. One could begin with an understanding of quantum light working and arrive at the same point. Sacred geometry is both basic and intricate. They are the same.

Sacred geometry is both a language and a formula, at once solved and unsolvable, for the layers with which one can interact are never-ending. That which one hears may not be recognized as a mathematical formula, but it is. That which you see with your eyes may not be recognized as interdimensional, but it is. This is the basis of sacred geometry.

I ask you, what color is 72? What is the basic enfoldment that will occur with that number into shape—or how does the angle of 72 begin to form itself into a shape? What is the emotion of 72? For it is distinct. Given that 72 has a basic numerical property, please understand that it will also have all other properties contained within it. For it exists. This is to tell you that in the basic structure of any number exists All That Is. Then it is to follow that the basic structure of any geometry contains the All That Is. This is why shapes and numbers have come to be associated with religions. They convey information and information always points back to creation, to God.

The All That Is within [you] gives the number and the shape their power to interact. It is a matter of their refinement. It is known that shape converts to numerical formula; yet numerical formula also converts to sound, sound converts to emotion, emotion to information, information to light, light to information, information to emotion, emotion to sound.

What looks like a circle in one dimension may be a line in another dimension as two points within that circle are activated into relationship. How does this occur? It is a vast interworking of the intention of All That Is creating electromagnetic communication, for those two points may contain the relationship that triggers the light, emotion, sound, or color needed for interaction. Forward that relationship comes, and the result is reality.

Once shape comes into being, the All That Is has already formed the idea, for it is the idea of the All That Is that brings forth reality. *Your free choice within this realm interacts with the idea of All That Is because you are not separate from All That Is.*

Clearly understand the force of choice, because you do have that ability. Know that within the scale of free choice you are choosing along with guidance from that aspect of you that is more closely aligned in vibration with All That Is [your Higher Self]. Most often humanity does not recognize the prompting of this guidance because it melds with you, as it has since your birth into this life.

Your choosing shapes geometries, and the geometries then shape the choosing.

As an absolute, that is as solid as it can be. Becoming comfortable in this will greatly enhance life experience and understanding as constants are variances. This is universal law. How else would growth continue? Allow understanding to be conceptual and you will expand. Only allowing understanding to be finite brings about decay.

In the vastness of All That Is, the same geometry will have different action depending on the person and the moment in time. Therefore, a square will have attributes and the interaction will vary by person. Such is the value of time; that you as a human may clarify which attribute comes forward into reality. For all attributes are activated—and within that which corresponds to the emotion, light, sound, color, time, and choice, the attributes are experienced. That is the reality of what you experience.

As you allow more conceptual experience, you will bring forth understanding of a vast array of the interaction, not just that which you see or hear. Begin to open to more of your senses. It is time.

The Language of Light is just as deeply layered with the sacred information of Life as geometry. Light Language opens the communication of profound Love, working through resistance and healing the deepest of wounds with relative ease. Through the magnetic power of Love, Light Language creates a new vibrational shape within your structure. It expands your mental constructs to access deeper layers of information than what is obvious or previously known.

Through the magnetic power of Love, Light Language creates a new vibrational shape within your structure.

The Language of Light creates deep change because rather than being moved through you at the pace of your belief structures, it moves at the speed of light as your lightbody communicates in the language of shape (also sound and light). Light Language allows humanity to move beyond the barriers that normal language imposes, as well as begin to experience a deeper communication with all of Life. It is a profound opening to heart-centered communication that honors all involved into a fuller potential of wisdom and evolution. It begins within you.

Chapter Seven

The Alchemy of Sound

Sound is a profound healer and connector. Sound and light are core aspects of life, like two sides of the same coin. Sound and light are both energy but perceived through different properties. An emanation of energy, intent, or consciousness creates a wave that is received through sight or hearing, depending on how the wave characteristic is received. Light waves are perceived differently than sound waves by the senses. Sound waves must have a carrier, like air or water molecules, to vibrate against and be interpreted into sound. The sound waves (also known as pressure waves) cause the eardrum to vibrate, and the brain interprets the vibration.

Just as with light, humans only hear within a certain spectrum. For instance, bats make constant noise when flying, using echolocation to "see" their reality. However, their sounds are outside of the spectrum of human hearing. Whether or not you hear a sound, the waves are present. Of course, sound waves affect more than your ear; they have a profound effect upon your whole body. The book *The Hidden Messages in Water* by Masaru Emoto is a wonderful reference work on the effect of sounds, though it more broadly covers the effect of intent, which can create sound. Emoto's work does not require speaking aloud to influence the shape of the water crystal.

Intent, the culmination of your perception, perspective, and choice, creates waves with a unique frequency, and the energy affects you. Emoto's work exemplifies that positive words (intent) create a harmonious water crystal, while negative words create a distorted water crystal. Your body is at least sixty-five percent water, so intent is always affecting the structure of the water in your body.

THE VISIBLE EFFECTS OF SOUND

Sound has been demonstrated to have a harmonizing and shaping effect in *Cymatics* by Hans Jenny. Jenny reveals the visible qualities of sound waves with sand on a drumhead. By changing the frequency of a sound, the geometry created by the waves is changed.

Sound has a deep effect on your health. It can help create harmony, release emotions, relax, or even amplify energy. Humanity has long used the power of sound to connect and heal. Whether through vocalization or an instrument, sound triggers memory, connection, and response. A mother singing to her baby is a powerful example of the connection and response sound creates. Even the timbre of a speaking voice influences a response beyond the meaning of the words; it can trigger associations that are unique to the history of an individual.

The power of music and the way it affects humans is a fascinating study. By examining the changes music has undergone in recent decades, you can make a generalization about the issues humanity has experienced during that time. Music isn't just a matter of taste; it is an indicator of the general energy flow of a person or a society. Some people only allow music to calm them and don't utilize its ability to increase energy. Others tune into the emotional aspects of words or music and allow that to elevate their energy, sometimes to the point of release through tears or anger. Other people do not allow the power of music to affect them strongly.

> ***Sound has a deep effect on your health. It can help create harmony, release emotions, relax, or even amplify energy.***

As you receive sound healing, even through the Language of Light, you may not know the details of how particular sounds are affecting the kidneys, for example. Yet sound (and the Language of Light) can certainly have an effect on them, as exemplified by Cymatics. The use of toning, chanting, singing and even speaking can all have a positive effect on many levels of healing. Sound is a powerful catalyst for change because of its deep physical and emotional effect.

The Emotional Effects of Sound

Tears are a common response I've observed to Light Language, because the information contained within it impacts the heart, which is a person's connection to Love and the vastness of Life. Many people think the Languages sound familiar even though they cannot understand their meaning. Even without the Language memory trigger, the frequency of the sound waves has a healing effect because of the extensive communication of Love embedded within them.

As exemplified by Emoto's water crystal photography and Jenny's Cymatics, the frequency of the information in Light Language has a restructuring effect. The impact of the waves creates a palpable ripple for those who are sensitive to feeling it. Just as one human feels cold in a certain temperature while another does not, Light Language is not perceived in the same way by everyone. However, the temperature (or the Language) is always there.

Movement affects you much the same way sound does. Imagine putting your finger in a still body of water and displacing the water, which then moves outward in ripples. As my body moves with the signing of Light Language, I am affecting the energy field of the client(s) I am working on. Light Language is a quantum communication beyond the limits of Newtonian physics (and time/space), so the client need not be in my presence to receive the healing benefits.

The Language of Light does not always need to be perceived as sound, but because of the multidimensional nature of Light Language, sound is always present—even if it is inaudible. Written words are silent, yet you hear them within. Written or signed Light Language is just as powerful as its audible forms. When you think in terms of receiving frequency into your energy field, you begin to realize information is being transmitted and received in many different ways. They are all beneficial. The five physical senses are receiving frequency and interpreting it into visible, audible, or sensory data for you. However, whether you are physically aware of the frequencies or not, they are there.

Sound is a powerful aspect of Life, and its study and usage is always beneficial. When you hear Light Language spoken or sung, you have the additional facet of profound energetic information being transmitted within sound. This helps you realize how deeply connected you are to Life. Hearing the Language of Light is like hearing the voice of Love speaking to you of the Love that you are. It changes you. For the better.

Chapter Eight

The Evolution of Language

The term Light "Language" often misleads people to believe it is linear, like human languages. Actual language is being transmitted, but it is not as limited to definitions as our Earth languages. In common languages, a word may have multiple agreed-upon meanings according to a dictionary. Everyone is taught definitions from an outside source, so we learn to communicate through pre-defined, agreed-upon sets of words.

This limitation is a beautiful aspect of the evolution of a species. From the separation of birth, humanity must learn to communicate. People naturally merge, diverge, and refine languages, sculpting them into something new that better matches the current human experience. Language defines a culture or society within a timeframe and separates it from other cultures or societies.

The beauty of Light Language is that the inhibitions of the mind are not activated by the mental and emotional triggers of words.

Light Language is a quantum leap into multi-dimensional communication. This is an exciting progression for humanity, as it indicates the beginnings of uniting into a form of full telepathic and empathic communication through the entire subtle sensory aspects of the energetic field. This is deeply connective, empowering, and heart-centered communication.

CREATIVE WORD

The Bible states that the word of God created the world, pointing to evidence of the power of word to create. Word is merely a focused, more specific, and denser form of idea, which is the beginning of creation. All word is creative, though often it is counteracted by unspoken belief or intent. The beauty of Light Language is that the inhibitions of the mind are not activated by the mental and emotional triggers of words.

For example, the word "love" may shut a person down as he or she dissociates because of pain correlated with love. *Light Language bypasses the mental and emotional limitations and speaks to the broader truth of Love.* Word, through the power of Light Language, is being recognized as far more than it previously was. The Language of Light is not just communication, which always has an effect; it is communion, connection, expansion, and evolution.

Language Origins

Human babies have a natural ability to mimic facial and sound expressions. This creates emotional bonding and safety with a parent. Verbal language, as well as body language, is connective for humans. However, there is no agreed-upon theory as to the beginning of spoken and written communication. I do not believe humanity developed them alone, but that is an extensive topic beyond the scope of this book.

> **The Language of Light is not just communication, which always has an effect; it is communion, connection, expansion, and evolution.**

I believe human languages developed from the understanding of the creative aspects of sounds, which were refined into meanings and words that were eventually represented in written form. *Words communicated the creational aspect of the energy of the sound, rather than just a definition of something external.*

For instance, rather than randomly choosing to call a leaf a leaf, I believe the sounds were correlated with the object's functionality in the broader scheme of life. Life. The *leaf* is a physical representation of the *life* of the plant. The leaf shows the flow of time, as is the case with all earthly life.

As one example, the Hebrew language has a rich connection to many details of the resonance of each sound/letter in the language. In the Hebrew language each letter, which would be better described as a sound rather than a letter, has a masculine or feminine quality. It also has a mathematical (numerological) correlation. There is much to be learned from studying linguistics, as well as paying attention to how you respond to words mentally and emotionally. As with any sound frequency, an effect creates a response.

Valuable Separation

In Hebrew and Sumerian historical writings, there are references to the idea that humanity was cast into speaking separate languages by God(s). The story of the Tower of Babel says that at one time, all of humanity spoke one language. They were building a tower to reach the heavens, and God became angry. God confused their language and dispersed them throughout the earth so they could no longer communicate with each other. The tower building stopped. To me, this allegory explains the descent of the human mind into lower evolution—also known as the "dark yugas" in Vedic traditions, as well as the fall of Atlantis (a broader discussion than this book can entail). Humans had a great ability to work together and create, but not the maturity to create responsibly. I believe the tower represents the hubris of corrupt power.

Distinct languages create group identities and isolate the group from those who do not know the language. This is beneficial to human diversity, as the language barrier helps establish individual and group identities. Separation is a natural part of human evolution; it fortifies people to a certain point, until unification becomes necessary to reach another level of strength.

Different areas of study or business develop jargon unique to their subject matter. Twins sometimes develop a unique language between themselves. Teenagers often develop or change words to have a specific meaning only to them, beginning a separation from their parents to identify more with their peers. They eventually establish personal strength and integrate more easily within many groups as adults. This separation process need not be a confrontational experience, yet as humanity heals its pain, separation often takes the form of bullying or cliques that vie for power over others. This will change as parents connect to their children more often with an empowered heart, rather than fear. This practice raises wiser children who feel less threatened by their environment and therefore are less likely to threaten others.

Distinct languages create a safety and unity—an identity—within a group that separates it from others; however, that is not necessarily a problem, merely an experience. As humanity evolves, the separation of groups will feel less threatening and be understood as a functionality of life. Diversity is a strength of nature. Through stages of development, groups begin to work together and find a new strength in unity. Language is a fascinating indicator of this separation and unity. Light Language brings connective communication to a new level.

Written Communication

There is no formal scientific agreement as to the origins of written language. It is generally believed that older written languages had a basis in symbols rather than specific letters that formed words, and words that formed specific, repeatable, identical sentences. Over time, people began to agree on meanings that were ascribed to words and letters, which refined language. The words were formed with an additive quality—root sounds had meanings that were built upon. Definitions were given by an external source, even if that source was collective agreement.

During the Dark Ages, the ability to read and write was reserved for religious establishments and nobility. As the Dark Ages progressed, religious institutions and the wealthy had the most control over what information the masses received. The wealthy had the privilege of education, while the masses did not. This created separation.

From the time when religions and nobles controlled the written word, humanity formed an agreement—though perhaps it was unconscious, or even forced—that what was written came from a trusted authority, outside of the self. People shared an unspoken expectation of superiority from the written word.

> *A person must hone his or her own discernment as to the validity of written or recorded content, rather than trusting without question that it has come from a responsible authority.*

    Accessibility to reading, writing, and printing changed this perception over time. First, the invention of the printing press made reproduction of text easier, and the Industrial Age made paper more easily available. The power of the printed word passed from nobility and religious institutions to commercial publishers, who determined what would or would not be allowed into mass distribution. The mainstream news is currently produced in this same way, with a few companies controlling all the information distributed on television and in print. The advent of the entertainment industry created yet another outlet for mass distribution. Still, much of humanity accepts these authorities as responsible, and the information as correct, without question.

    The Internet has made it possible for individuals to mass distribute information without any established or formal authority. This is a great advancement for the empowerment of humanity. It also creates a new and extremely valuable problem. *A person must hone his or her own discernment as to the validity of written or recorded content, rather than trusting without question that it has come from a responsible authority.* Many still blindly believe what they see and read, even when evidence to the contrary is presented.

The Language of Light also requires personal discernment of what is appropriate for your own needs. Because there is no established authority outside of the self (there is no agreed-upon dictionary), each individual must learn to follow their own instincts of what is transmitting and being received. It is a new empowerment with communication, reflected in the current state of information flow.

CONNECTIVE LANGUAGE

You may be aware that when you speak and listen to language, there is much more going on than just the words you hear. You can observe both body language and tone of voice, otherwise known as nonverbal communication. These indicate the intent of the speaker and can be discerned by instinct. Many people predominantly listen to words, not utilizing and trusting their natural intuitive senses regarding nonverbal communication. As humanity learns to utilize its innate intuition, it will more easily discern the unspoken intent behind audible words. For instance, one who intends to manipulate with the words, "I love you," may be able to manipulate one person but not another. When utilized, the intuitive senses are astute to the vibrational harmony or disharmony of words and intent.

Intent brings a multilayered quality to common words. *However, Light Language does not originate from the human mind, so the Language is not layered with the totality of the human's intent.* Light Language allows for a deeper and purer internal connection with others because of the higher frequency of the information. This access into innate wisdom is an important aspect of what Light Language indicates for humanity's development. Outside groups can no longer as easily determine with absolute authority what you hear, see, and interpret to be true or false. *Each person is required to connect and discern in order to understand the truth of what is presented.*

Transitioning Beyond Linear Language

The Language of Light is a communication with the Higher Self, the more subtle aspect of self. It is a broad, unifying, and multidimensional form of communication, as is your Higher Self. The human challenge of it is opening to an understanding of the subtle realms, anchoring them here on Earth and not repeating old patterns of interaction. *Humanity is opening to a new quality of empowered communication and Light Language is a core bridge for this.*

The Language of Light is vast information in a wave form packet of invisible light.

Some Light Language is more linear or defined than others, but Light Language is multidimensional. This concept is a hard one to grasp; humans are most familiar with linear progression as fact. I am often asked, "What does this word mean?" However, Light Language does not generally translate as linearly or specifically as human languages. It contains vast information and healing frequencies within it, so a translation will vary, though it will always contain a thread of continuity.

I had an experience of translating written Light Language that detailed a certain technology that creates a magnetic field of propulsion. I was told someone else gave the same translation. To an outside eye, the Light Language looked like what could be described as writings vaguely similar to Sanskrit. Yet two people who never met were able to derive the same unique (though not verbatim) translation.

You, like all humans, are accustomed to deriving meaning from agreement and context. You are not accustomed to allowing the vastness to remain undefined *and* understood. This is where paradox meets expansion. The understanding that Light Language can be both undefined and understood indicates a next step in the evolution of humanity. *As humans move into higher-frequency expression, we are required to become empowered individuals in order to support and sustain connection, rather than disempowered individuals who only give power to an outside authority.* To connect into a group (the vastness), an individual must be strong enough to handle the physical, mental, emotional, and spiritual difference without losing empowerment.

Speaking in Tongues

There are references to Light Language, a natural capability for humanity, in many ancient manuscripts, religious texts and shamanic practices throughout the world. People often ask if the Language of Light is the same as speaking in tongues, which is generally a western religious reference that originated from multiple biblical mentions. While various religious sects experience speaking in tongues, the Pentecostals have practiced this for many years and are perhaps some of the best known for maintaining this capability. The Pentecostals were often depicted with fire and a halo above their head, representing their developed crown chakra. The fire represents divine language capability and correlates with the neural patterning that creates an amplified firing of neurons due to an intensified transmission of information. *The Keys of Enoch* also makes reference to fire letters.

Light Language and speaking in tongues are the same, and yet, distinct in some ways. In both, a person is able to channel information verbally in a language unknown to them (glossolalia or xenoglossia). The difference with Light Language is in the frequencies and information that are now more accessible and discernable, such as galactic and elemental energies. Speaking in tongues has a long history that is generally unknown or misunderstood and spans many cultures. It has allowed humanity to maintain an ability that is now expanding outside of a religious or shamanic context.

When I first began channeling the Language of Light, it was through my hands as I silently signed it over the bodies of my energy healing clients. I had never been exposed to it or even heard of it. I had heard of speaking in tongues, but I had never experienced it directly. When I asked my Guides what was happening, I was expecting healing information about the client. Instead I was told the number of people on Earth who "do this." The number was too small to include all of the people who were speaking in tongues. As I discovered over the next few years, it was an indicator of the number of people who were opening to channel frequencies that are distinct from speaking in tongues, such as galactic energies.

__Humanity is opening to a new quality of empowered communication and Light Language is a core bridge for this.__

It is important for humanity to honor what is being built upon without falling into the natural tendency to denigrate it. Light Language is not better or more evolved than speaking in tongues. It is just a new term for a related concept that indicates the overall evolution of humanity. As humanity evolves, the availability of the Language of Light increases to reflect the acceleration of the Christed consciousness—the ability of a person to live in unity and Love with all of Life. *The Book of Knowledge: The Keys of Enoch* by JJ Hurtak has many references to the Language of Light being a Language those of a certain consciousness level will be able to speak. Humanity as a whole is moving into fourth-density physicality (also known as fourth- and fifth-dimensional expression), which is a more conscious state that will be discussed in a later chapter.

Light Language and speaking in tongues are similar, distinct, and two definitions for communicating with the Divine. The paradox of the parts containing the whole, the fractal nature of life, expands the mind beyond mere separation.

Quantum Language

Light Language is not a defined language—it is quantum language. It is called the Language of Light because language is information and light is a quantum "packet" with the potential to exhibit both wave-like and particle-like properties. Since there are little to no preconceived or defined terms within Light Language, the information is received in wave form rather than particle form. *The Language of Light is vast information in a wave form packet of invisible light.* This light is beyond the spectrum of sight and therefore is not affected by the perceptions of sight. It interacts with the physical body and the subtle body in its full wave form.

A wave form, as indicated through the Observer Effect, is malleable to intent; this is why the effect of Light Language changes with each listener or each repeated listening. The Higher Self is more available to interact with the healing frequencies without the interference of human resistance or confusion. The Light Language frequencies transmit healing information to the body, which the Higher Self immediately receives and instructs. This creates the particle light response within the process as it becomes specific to the person receiving it in the moment. Thus, the Language of Light is quantum information unique to the observer in the moment.

> ***The Language of Light calls the human heart into power and connects it with the mind.***

Due to its quantum nature, Light Language is a holistic communication. It directly interacts with your Lightbody, initiating change within your most subtle and creative aspect. Because there is an innate, heart-centered recognition of it, Light Language automatically fires creation memories, or "divine blueprint" neurons in the physical brain. I believe that our ancient languages, especially their written form, had a basis in the light patterns the brain creates as it transmits neural impulses. These sparks are the catalyst for new neural imprinting and the release of negative brain patterning habits. This new patterning, in turn, releases different hormones in the body than the previous patterns created, resulting in changes to your physical experience over time.

TELEPATHIC COMMUNICATION

Light Language begins an opening of human telepathic channels. It is not just a direct telepathic transmission of a single thought; it interacts directly with your overall intuitive receptors, rather than your physical mental capacities which hear words, tone of voice and interprets their meaning. Light Language is a bridge to fuller telepathic communication that eventually will be transmitted without sound or shape. In its current audible and visible form, we are reaching beyond learned communication by blending linear and non-linear experience and understanding. Your telepathic abilities may include hearing another's thoughts (mental empathy), feeling another's emotions (emotional empathy), or even feeling another's physical experience (physical empathy). Light Language is a full telepathic experience, not just a mental telepathic transference.

In order to have the ability to perceive telepathic data and remain focused in love and compassion, you must be a mentally and emotionally strong, balanced individual. As we blend the linearity of human language and the non-linearity of Light Language, we are learning to receive fuller communication. Each individual must learn empowerment so humanity can interact without manipulation or agendas driven by greed and fear. Empowerment is the core of evolution, and empathy is fundamental to telepathic connection.

When I transmit Light Language, I am aware of multiple streams of information. At times I hear transmissions within, while I hear another transmission out loud. Sometimes I clairvoyantly see additional Light Language streams transmitting from my mouth, (as well as my eyes, hands, and body), though I cannot hear it. It is a purely telepathic transmission that involves the whole being. It is our conscious, linear mind that limits what can be perceived, but this is a beneficial and natural progression of weaving the vast unconscious functionality with the linear conscious details.

HUMANITY EVOLVES

Eventually everyone will understand and speak Light Language. It is beginning a change in the way that all humans interact as we open to higher-frequency communication. Each person must become more personally responsible and connected with the universe. Humanity is recognizing a direct connection with God and that all beings are an aspect of God. Your ability to discern what is right for you, and to trust your own judgment when something is not, is a powerful lesson that Light Language helps to anchor. The Language of Light brings the external of Life (God, angels, galactic beings, other humans, etc.) into the internal as humanity begins to communicate on a more connective and universal scale.

The Language of Light calls the human heart into power and connects it with the mind. With that, you expand your ability to communicate and understand; you interact differently and the world changes. Light Language is a catalyst in the evolution of humanity's ability to communicate and connect. It is a profound advancement of communication with the Higher Self—and even beyond that into multidimensional awareness and communication with life beyond the human experience.

Section Three

Light Language: Interaction

Multidimensional Life

This section helps you understand humanity's connection with the subtle realms and how this relates to your personal Light Language journey. We begin with an understanding of multidimensionality, the dimensions, and Ascension to establish a context of the changes that are occurring for humanity, which Light Language indicates and enhances. This section next details how Light Language works directly with your DNA through your Higher Self, heart, brain, ego, and intent.

Chapter Nine

Overview of Multidimensionality

Multidimensional life refers to the concept of life on a greater scale than what humanity was previously aware of or interacted with before. Technically, humans always were and always will be interacting with multiple dimensional structures. The term "dimension" in this context is a mix of scientific terminology (length, width, depth, and the measurement of time) and esoteric information. Even the scientific definitions of dimensions vary as they pertain to different fields of science.

In this section, I use the terms "dimension" and "dimensional expression" to bring some cohesive perception and clarity to the way the term is generally used in spiritual discussion. The term "dimensional expression" is used to emphasize that dimensions (as discussed in the context of Ascension) are definitions and rules of expression that humans observe. Dimensions are directly related to perspective. Vibrational data is interpreted with the five physical senses of sight, sound, smell, taste, and touch. There are senses beyond these five that connect humanity to a less defined reality, or dimensional expression. These are often referred to as higher dimensions. Higher dimensions are just higher frequencies not generally perceptible to our physical senses.

The discussion of dimensions can be framed through varied categorizations, terminologies, and subsets. It can be purely mathematical, mechanical, or metaphorical, but I believe it should apply to life fairly obviously. *Dimensions are merely accepted rules of delineation*, so in essence the definitions of them are arbitrary, though helpful.

There are senses beyond the five senses that connect humanity to a less defined reality, or a higher-frequency dimensional expression.

Dimensions are not separable in the sense that one stops and another begins. They are interdependent and interacting with one another at all times. However, until you become aware, you will not notice their implications in your life. As you become more aware of what is contained within length, width, and depth (the visible), you find that time (though invisible in and of itself—we can only observe its effect) is a marker of manifestation. Form does not exist without time in this realm, and thus, any form is a distinct moment(s) in time.

Density or Dimension?

Some channels talk about humanity moving from third density to fourth density instead of defining Ascension as a dimensional progression. Dimensions are your observation of the world around you and the rules within which it is defined. The definitions of the densities are a foundational necessity because rather than defining what is around you, they define *your* physical and subtle biomechanism. There are seven defined densities of physical life. A wonderful overview of this can be found in *The Prism of Lyra* by Lyssa Royal Holt.

The way in which your biomechanism reacts with the dimensional rules around you is what many channelers refer to as the dimensions. In actuality, your density changes as you become more based in Love, unity, and connection rather than fear or domination. As your physical density changes, you become aware of new rules that were always around you, and you are able to interact with them more readily. This is the core of consciousness. As you become more conscious of Love or transform from fear, you become more conscious of the dimensional expressions around you and your interaction with them becomes more conscious.

To summarize, humanity is moving from third density to fourth density. This defines your physical and subtle structure. Fourth density is a less-dense physical expression, though it can look the same to the physical senses. Within fourth density are new rules of interaction with the world around you; this new interaction is arbitrarily termed the fourth and fifth dimensions (and higher). The fourth and fifth dimensions are higher-dimensional expressions than humanity previously had conscious access to with its third density bodies and minds. Evolution is naturally expanding your abilities. Yet part of that work is within each individual, for the choice to change comes from within. As you align more with your Loving, empowered nature, you progress your physical structure into fourth density, a higher-dimensional interactive vehicle.

Lower and Higher Dimensions

The lower dimensions (to a certain frequency range) are more visible or palpable to our senses. For example length, depth, and width are palpable, yet time is only observable from its effects. The lower dimensions are not less evolved; they are merely part of the building blocks of physical reality. Earth itself has a lower density vibration; however, as a consciousness, Earth/Gaia is extremely evolved. The visible aspect of that statement can be proven; the invisible aspect, that Earth has a consciousness, cannot be proven with our current scientific methods and instruments. Some would then say it does not exist, just as humans first had difficulty believing that microscopic germs exist. It is the same with dimensions; there is no current proof for much of what humans are beginning to understand, so it requires your internal discernment of what feels appropriate to you, in addition to your logic.

> *When your current vibration interacts with a higher vibration, you begin a process of entrainment that surfaces the emotional, mental, and physical vibrations that are not in resonance with the higher vibration you have accessed.*

As your vibration rises into a higher frequency, which is more resonant with Love and your Christed consciousness, you have more access to interact with the higher dimensions. It is as simple as your higher-dimensional sensory capabilities, the intuitive senses, becoming more available to you. Light Language is an exciting part of the interaction with higher dimensions that humanity is experiencing, though it is not the only way to access it.

The Language of Light helps bring an expanded experience of communication, not only between humans who interact with it, but with higher-dimensional nonhuman beings who interact through Loving agreement of assistance with humanity's evolution. Your individual cosmic heritage, whether angelic, galactic, and/or elemental, is connecting with you and communicating, just as your Earth heritage is. This communication impacts the vibration on Earth through your free will and your soul path.

Multidimensional Progression

Expanding into higher-dimensional interaction is most often gradual, though it usually involves short, exciting experiences of new access. At first they are unique and rather different from what you are accustomed to experiencing, like a powerful vision or a loving experience with an Angel. These experiences give you something tangible, a sense of capability, and even hope that you can continue accessing the connective higher dimensions.

How you deal with "coming back to reality" helps you access the higher dimensions more easily. When your current vibration interacts with a higher vibration, you begin a process of entrainment that surfaces the emotional, mental, and physical vibrations that are not in resonance with the higher vibration you have accessed. Here you have a choice to suppress and avoid them, or release and transform them. This will determine how much higher you are able to go, or how often you are able to access higher dimensions. Releasing past pain and trauma is a valuable part of your journey of Ascension (rapid evolution).

As you become more interactive with your multidimensional nature, you expand your awareness of "reality." The new dimensions you will be able to access have an additive effect. *You are not replacing earthly life with another dimensional expression; you are augmenting human capability.* You, as one interested in Light Language and other forms of healing and expansion, are a forerunner of this integration.

> **You are not replacing earthly life with another dimensional expression; you are augmenting human capability.**

Your multidimensional expansion will integrate gradually into your life, though the progress may feel abrupt at times. There will be quiet times of integration, which are vital to your rejuvenation. There will also be less obvious, perhaps even challenging, movement that stretches you to see past the exciting (sometimes addictive) upgrades. It may challenge you at times, but it will always exalt you if you continue to move forward with it.

Chapter Ten

The Dimensions

A higher frequency is also what many refer to as a higher dimension. Many channelers are now talking about the fourth and fifth dimensions (or more). Some say humanity is moving into them, or already has, or is in and out of them, and so on. Some of that information is correct and some is incorrect. Use your discernment. Essentially these channelers mean that when your frequency (your density) is higher, you have access to congruent information and experiences that are of a higher frequency, or a less dense structure.

From my perspective, fourth-dimensional expression is a personal mastery of time, manifestation, and the subtle realms. It is the ultimate sovereignty. In essence, it is duality balanced into a strength of interaction with form rather than polarization, avoidance, or domination. As an example, fourth-dimensional mastery would be indicated by not getting impatient when things are difficult or not the way you imagined. As you understand the flow of time with no fear of lack polarizing you, you remain neutral to circumstances, knowing all is well and constantly changing. As fourth-dimensional integration occurs, you may have moments of fear, but they are easily replaced with an authentic sense of wellbeing. This happens more quickly as you strengthen your knowing of your capability as a Divine human.

You naturally interact with all dimensions. The difference is in awareness and emphasis.

Fifth-dimensional expression is personal mastery of the connective nature of Life, which is Love in its many forms. One who has mastered fifth-dimensional expression feels no revulsion toward humans who behave in destructive ways, for the greater evolutionary potential is known deeply within. The self is understood to be connected to All Life, and therefore it does not judge another, even as it understands a behavior as destructive. When interacting with "lower vibrating humans," there is no judgment, derision, or desire to suppress others. Love is not always pleasant on the earthly plane, but a person of fifth-dimensional mastery views the human challenge through the lens of the connective force of Love, which embraces and offers healing without a need to overpower. The true power of Love is known and fostered within, and Love's potential is seen within every being and experience.

Within both fourth- and fifth-dimensional expressions, sovereignty and individual identity still exist. Within both there is still duality, but as a non-negative experience of life in human form. There is no bursting into light and oneness, or going somewhere bad people are not allowed; *it is evolved human expression*.

Many traditions speak of humans transforming into light, such as Elijah's transfiguration in the Bible. That process differs from the evolutionary experience of Ascension humanity is embarking upon at this time. Humanity as a whole species is moving into fourth density, where the subtle realms begin to be more accessible. This change initiates access to higher dimensions such as fourth- and fifth-dimensional expressions.

You Are Multidimensional

Life is intelligently designed for its own continuation and progression. *You naturally interact with all dimensions. The difference is in awareness and emphasis.* The connective heart and delineative brain help you determine how to expand and interact more adeptly with the next level of progression as it pertains to your life. Early humans became more adept at feeding and sustaining themselves through a growing understanding of nature. Agriculture and cooperation with others brought great strides to the joy of life. These improvements were always available; it just took the progression of time for people to understand their potential through observation and action.

The following channeled message about dimensional expression is one such guide. It is framed from human understanding and heart/brain capacity and expansion. It is esoteric, symbolic, and rich with unspoken meaning and encodements that your brilliant heart/mind will unfold. Allow yourself to enjoy the flow of the information and know you are taking it in on more levels than you may first consciously realize, through the filter of your Higher Self. Please note that any misspelled words in this section are intentional and enhance the meaning of the word. Sometimes grammatically incorrect punctuation may be used to navigate the pace or flow of information.

> Prior to dimensional expression is potential, the All. This is the most mind-boggling part, the reason that all time is now and that all is, has been and always will be. It is the time and timeless within the same totality. It is represented by the zero in your numerical system. It holds no place and yet everything is within it. It holds no marker until form has formed and keeps forming. Potential is the vessel from which all manifestation is birthed. It is the pre-beginning that comes from the begun. The circle. The circle is not visible from within, yet all is within it. The circle is visible from beyond, but what is within it remains

hidden until birth, then only part of it discernable to the outside. This zero dimension is the becoming, until it has become. Then it becomes the zero point. Life, as dimensions, builds upon it. It is not gone, it is formed. Beyond the bubble of potential, the butterfly emerges. The zero, the All, becomes the point, the One.

The first dimension is the point. **Po**ten-tial **int**o form. It is idea in its subtle form, it is word in its denser form, it is matter in its densest form. Even within the densification of matter, there is no end to internal potential and external progress. The inception is the inner potential becoming outer manifest as subtle and denser never stop their dance. The flow of Life is continual in all directions. The brain expands as the heart reaches out, reaches in, and reaches out farther again. The inner and outer converge within the point. As you get the point you give the progress, and Life's engine of movement continues. The direction is the culmination of potential meeting choice and the inner begins its movement through time as the unknown, unrecognized, unrevealed dimensions fold and furl through space. Through time it is a lifetime and yet not a second, but the direction has its motion.

The second dimension is direction. This offers the beauty of reflection and the ugliness of separation recognized. With deeper reflection and broader direction, the inner and outer expand in all directions, beginning the inclusion of all excluded through separation. The line has been crossed, the cross has been maligned, and where the two shall meet is the trinity of divinity recognized. It is direction upon which information flows, having mattered so much that form gathers to it. The folding, the furling; here it is unseen movement as the separation begins to revile that separation is revealed. Direction needs fuel, as motion is energy. One must but tap into the limitless potential within, the zero point directed; and direction continues its flow. Until containment, the bubble, the event horizon, the limitation, the skin of containment is met. Is it death, is it depth, how deep does it go? From this point, moving in direction, what is beyond is unknown. The direction has changed, folded in upon itself and met with reflection. The line has now crossed the line of duality into the triad of new beginning.

The third dimension is the depth of containment, the bubble aware, the potential within realized and birthed. Self is now observing itself as the direction has moved it beyond to the next, for it has context; the next container. The bubble was a limitation and a liberation, not so limited as first believed. The beauty of the third is realized through the eyes of direction, just as ugliness is also a choice point. Folding in and furling out man's infestation of self is flying free for realization. How will this potential be directed? Only Time will tell, as its whisper is now being heard. *When it speaks of what is beyond, who understands its foreign words?* Slowly at first, for Time reveals through direction traversed; the words begin to make sense. When the reflection is loud and the in-turned chatter even louder, who will follow the path of Time's wisdom? Who will go that deep, for it is a death of sorts. The circle continues.

The fourth dimension evens out the odds, as each layer of visible and invisible is revealed. What seems odd in three becomes even in "we." Time heals all wounds. Time is the master weaver; it threads the paths and looms the fabric of space. In the fourth dimension the understanding of movement is released, as choice moves beyond the boundary conditions of what is known into the trust of Knowing the unknown. Here all directions converge and explode out, marking paths of progress for the next contained to choose. There are conditions, though. For the information does not lie, it flows.

As conditions of the boundaries are met, it requires boundless flow to move beyond. Acquiesce to Time and the fullness of the contained is revealed as the expansion beyond is propelled. The zero point directed contains all and more. What is beyond is One and All. Wonderful. As it always was.

The fifth dimension is the unified equations. All points have expanded and contracted into the perfection of the circle. Time has revealed the full picture of the unity within the potential points. The One and the All are separate and knot. The dark and the light are different and same. The good and the bad are always both. The reflection is the play of shadows and color. Connection becomes visible to those with eyes to see. Two see beyond the duality, one must connect to All, the manifestation of four and one is five. The *foreign* one is clear. The limitless, boundless, infinite All is contained, understood, ingested, and released. Time has passed the marker to the maker. Creation begins. Again.

The sixth dimension is the elixir. As you sense its sweetness limit is revealed as limitless. There is no love that is not lost and found, there is no loss that is not gained. There is only every thing and no thing. The sixth dimension is the compeller and expeller, the true engine of continuance. The container is in you. The container is contained. Liberation is an inside job. The inner and the outer meet at a point of potential and new direction begins. Here is the secret to All Life, for its brilliance and beauty will blind and belie until the full information and connection is complete. Exhausted, exhilarated they are but the smallest of points as the grand unseen is the most visible of All. All that came before it is only because of it. The becoming of it is the infinite within the finite; the unendable ending and beginning again. In the sixth dimension the paradox of duality is ingested, digested, and spun out into the circle of Life. Love the process, for it is All. 0 to 6D indicates that all is connected and stems from the same Source. One never existed without six already existing, yet how did six begin? The linearity of direction has been revealed as all directions. It is merely perspective.

The seventh dimension is Earth on heaven, with perspective revealing the true nature of Life. Here, with the cast of subtlety met, there is no beginning or ending, just meeting the moment in its full information. The power of Love is but a mere mechanism that is so pure its system is known. There is no other, for purity prevails. Rather than purity being one thing, it is All in balance. Within the seventh heaven finality is the beginning of connection birthed. The fracture is fractal and factual in form, for there is the fact of Love's permeation and permutation repeating. There is no other, for Love is such mastery that it is mastered. Its truth of manipulation is manufactured, the fractal fractured but never broken. This opening, we come full circle. Direction is revealed. The mental meanderings of men means little to the master of Love. Connection, it seams, is direction; and perspective is both. There is no line or circle that is not both. Heaven is revealed.

The eighth dimension is ether ore, for elemental discoveries are eternally in evolution. This engine of movement is the folding in, the furling out, the fractal movement moving. Timeless is stillness as movement is eternal. The invisible engine of inner outer revealed. Forging ahead we know already and yet all is unknown. Life is compelled to movement and stillness reveals Life's mystery. The infinite Loving is so vast that it feels far away. All has moved through it, for all is within it, yet everything is its own without. It is the container, yet it knows that if all is contained within, there must be a without. For infinity is all and eternity is ever turning. The circle begins.

But what of potential? The ninth dimension begets eternity, yet potential must already exist for potential to exist. The framework of start and finish is completed and the furling births the folding. How did the end come before the beginning? The two are connected, yet two indicates separation. Infinity is available to your mind of limitation, for it is within limitation that freedom is boundary-less. All life is within, the system is complete, and completion is a point of newness.

This mysterious discussion of the dimensions is meant to help you expand your mind into a conceptual understanding of the invisible engine of Life. Did you notice a pattern evolving? As the dimensions increased in number there was a reflection of previous dimensions, and they became more esoteric as the numbers increased.

Multidimensional Awareness

Light Language helps expand your dimensional awareness by raising your vibration to a higher frequency. In the previous channeling about the third dimension (the dimensional expression readily accepted by the scientific community, though many scientists also consider time to be the fourth dimension), there was a reference to our Ascension and to Light Language that I became aware of while editing this book. It states: "Folding in and furling out, man's infestation of self is flying free for realization. How will this potential be directed? Only time will tell, as its whisper is now being heard. *When it speaks of what is beyond, who understands its foreign words?* Slowly at first, for Time reveals through direction traversed; the words begin to make sense."

I chose to italicize that sentence in the channeling, as well as the reference to it in the section about the fifth dimension, because it points to the power of Light Language, "its whisper now being heard" as we communicate beyond known and limited words. The "foreign words" point to fourth- and fifth-dimensional expression, as well as the Language of Light seeming foreign to the mind. Light Language is a fifth-dimensional (and higher) form of communication, though people will be drawn to it as they access fourth-dimensional expression. The Language of Light is a doorway to humanity's Ascension, and it is an exciting one!

What many on the path of Ascension are experiencing is access to higher-dimensional expression at different times. First you may experience it only during meditation, then perhaps out in nature, then perhaps in a few more settings. It begins to occur more frequently, but at first it's not consistent. Often there is an integration phase and later another clearing phase as you release discordant vibrations, perceptions, and choices. It's a process. With a supportive perspective, it can be fascinating.

> *Your path of healing and empowerment changes your sensory perception into greater access with the higher vibrating dimensional structures.*

The progress of your multidimensionality will be similar to the experiences of others and it will be unique to you because of your distinct perspective. Each being and each experience is valuable information that calls humanity toward improvement. This is the benefit of challenge—it strengthens resolve, sharpens focus, and grows authentic personal empowerment. The unwanted challenges stir your desire to create anew. It calls you to live life powerfully. Self-love is imperative. It shapes the lens through which you perceive others and Life.

As you progress into higher-dimensional expression, you will gradually begin to interact with time, rather than just respond to it. The pace of life will feel exhilarating yet balanced. You will remember that play and patience are vital to your wellbeing. As you continue your healing and empowerment, you will gradually begin to create with Love, rather than seek to feel it from another. You will show yourself and others the power of forgiveness and the power of holding a boundary that supports Love's growth. You will feel a deep connection to life that has no lack, no desperation—even as you improve. You will know that all is well and progressing perfectly, for the engine of Life is fail-safed to Love. As you recognize that you *are* Love, you connect with All of Life through your awareness of that powerful Truth.

Your path of healing and empowerment changes your sensory perception into greater access with the higher vibrating dimensional structures. You expand your awareness of the dimensional interactions, broader frequencies, and the invisible engine of Life. You become the multidimensional being you always were, but that humanity is evolving into through the vehicle of physical form.

Through Light Language, I have expanded my own understanding of the connection I have to other realms of existence. My knowledge has unfolded as I seek to apply a higher-dimensional expression into the life challenges and triumphs I am experiencing. As you access your innate ability to expand beyond what you have known, you will find Light Language to be a powerful bridge of connection for your Ascension.

Chapter Eleven

Ascension
(Polarity Integration)

Ascension is merely a term that refers to humanity's natural evolution into awareness of higher-frequency vibration. Ascension increases your ability to discern and consciously interact with higher-dimensional expressions. You develop skills like transmitting Light Language—communicating with loving angelic, galactic, or elemental beings. You become more peaceful, creative, and empowered in life.

As you move beyond survival fears, your brain develops new capacities (though these capacities were always there) and you focus on details of life beyond the five physical senses. Ascension is a broad topic, but it is inherent to the evolution of humans and it is unfolding at a more rapid pace than ever before.

Humanity is moving into fourth density, which is an integrated interaction with fourth- and fifth-dimensional expression. These dimensional rules have always been there and interacted with humanity, but as humanity progresses, these dimensional criteria become known and actively co-creative. This is the reason there is currently so much focus on creating your reality with your thoughts and feelings as part of a spiritual path; you are learning to work more directly with the powerful engine of the subtle realms.

Ascension is the equivalent of anchoring the frequency of the Higher Self with the human Self.

Ascension requires each person to access their inner empowerment, thereby balancing their independent and interdependent natures. It requires the ego structure to be fluid and strong (not to be confused with control, which is fear-based). It is a state of active participation with the Divine Creator within, while maintaining an empowered, sovereign, and connected interaction with All Life.

As humanity is now experiencing it, Ascension is not an immediate dissolving into Light, nor is it the rescue and removal of good humans from Earth. It is a natural process of human evolution that brings awareness of and interaction with higher-dimensional rules as the human frequency is raised to a higher, less dense frequency (fourth density). Remember not to polarize into the belief that higher dimensions are good and lower dimensions are bad; they are merely the building blocks of form and consciousness.

Ascension is the equivalent of anchoring the frequency of the Higher Self with the human Self. This creates an empowered sovereign individual who interacts with unity consciousness; you see beyond the obvious separation of duality and into the connective nature of Life. It is the pinnacle of cooperation, creating win-win scenarios in all aspects of earthly life. It is an honoring reflected in many ancient teachings; respect the earth and All Life upon her, including yourself.

Light Language, along with many other valuable techniques and tools, assists the process of Ascension as the ego releases control. The Divine mind comes online and the heart takes its lead role in the human experience. Your brilliant mind then applies heart wisdom to the earth experience. From interacting with Light Language for my own healing and growth, I released conscious and unconscious trauma from my past, and fear of the future. I then had more access to peace, joy, and a new perspective of hope. Not in every moment, but enough to recognize the difference as it grew. I began to appreciate life more and see the human experience through a more loving perspective. It isn't a quick process, but you are worth the effort.

The Language of Light is an effective catalyst for Ascension because it naturally conveys information of connection, which then unfolds from within you. This empowers you as you discover your innate intelligence. Each person has a unique perspective, and the distinctive information they receive and emit is valuable to the progression of Life as a whole. Ascension elevates these perspectives to the empowered, loving truth of Life's potential as humanity opens to the unseen, yet vast, information of Life. It starts within you.

The Yugas

The timing of each individual's Ascension is as unique as the individual, but there is a collective timing to the process as well. Many ancient cultures have recorded the cycles of time in such great detail that even pyramids in Egypt and across South America have been shown to be intricately aligned with time cycles. Ancient Hindu writings chronicle the yugas, the epochs that define the progression of life. The Mayan calendar also tracked larger and smaller cycles that have come out of focus in the Western world. Rather than the world ending, as was often portrayed prior to the "ending" of the Mayan calendar on December 21, 2012, it was merely marking the end of a large cycle of about 25,900 years. Yet like every ending, it overlaps with beginnings.

Earth moves through the universe, intimately tied to the Milky Way galaxy and also locked into magnetic movement with the surrounding galaxies and heavenly bodies. The photonic radiation and magnetic movement, the push/pull, influences humanity's physical, emotional, and mental bodies as evolution persists. As Earth crossed through the galactic center on December 21, 2012, it completed a long cycle as shown by the

Mayan calendar. The intensified magnetic resonance of the galactic center shapes the beingness of humanity. This, along with the intent of individual humans, is a powerful catalyst for evolution. This cosmic dawning, which does not occur in one day, has the effect of awakening your innate knowledge of your cosmic and divine nature.

Polarity Integration is merely a function of evolution and takes a natural course.

Humanity is currently experiencing an *ascending* phase from the Iron Age (also known as the Kali Yuga) into the Bronze Age (Dvapara Yuga). This time marks an integration of innate feminine energy that has been suppressed. As you awaken your innate divinity, suppression and separation are no longer tenable. Each being is born imbued with masculine and feminine energy, regardless of gender. As you heal and progress into your wholeness, you are naturally compelled to unity consciousness. Unity consciousness requires empowered (inner powered) individuals to maintain a cohesive diversity that benefits All Life.

Reunification

The separation of masculine and feminine is the macro-separation. Humanity separates into many different categories, or micro-separations, but this is the top-tier separation of the individual. It is the core of the duality experience. The balancing of your internal masculine and feminine energies is the secret to expansion, though it has nothing to do with whether or not you are male or female. Instead it is your balance of directing (masculine energy) and allowing (feminine energy) with life that matters. It affects how you create in all aspects of your life. It is Polarity Integration.

Your ability to both direct and allow as you co-create your life is what anchors the experience of empowered individuals cooperating within a group. Each group connects with other groups and the cycle strengthens, improves, and expands. The micro-separation of different groups changes from opposition to cooperation. An individual is required to be empowered from within (sovereign), then to interact in new ways, thus exponentially influencing the healing of others.

> **Moving past the judgment of duality and into its potential connection is what elevates humans.**

All of this is esoteric; it is not yet accepted by science. Polarity Integration is merely a function of evolution and takes a natural course. There is an interplay of light and dark within life on Earth, which manifests as "good" or "bad" through human perception. As humanity evolves, everyone will begin to realize the potential engine of expansion this opposition imposes and will then recognize that it is merely two sides of the same coin. This theoretical coin of duality exists within All Life on Earth.

Moving past the judgment of duality and into the embracing of its potential connection is what elevates humans beyond the limitations of third density into fourth density, as well as to fourth- and fifth-dimensional expression. That elevation requires a balanced and empowered connection within the self, with others, and with the totality of Life itself. This is Ascension.

Evolution

As humanity moves into higher-dimensional expression, Life adjusts and changes. There is no giant leap of extreme difference; rather, change evolves through the appropriate seasons. The physical body changes. The habits of eating, exercising, rest, play, relationships, and sexuality change. Every aspect of Life becomes whole, connective, creative, and loving. Any unseen agendas or insecurities are compassionately exposed to each person for resolution.

Each human being is given an opportunity to recognize and release any blocks to actualizing empowered Love. Your soul may press a little harder if you don't hear the call to Love, but all experience is an opportunity to evolve. As you learn to listen to the quiet voice within yourself and the communication of what your life experiences are teaching you, you become adept at seeing blocks when they are less challenging and easier to resolve.

Ascension

The Language of Light, as it transmits core information of Love, reveals to each individual an inherent connection to the Source of Life. As you recognize your own divinity, you begin to perceive Life through the filter of the Love of God. In this way, you begin to truly connect with Life on Earth through the lens of Love.

> True Love does not compete; it complements.
>
> True Love does not resist the misgivings of humanity; it holds a Knowing that all humans are continually in a process of learning the details of Love.
>
> True Love does not mourn death; it recognizes transformation.
>
> True Love does not overpower; it nurtures the flourishing of life.

This is Ascension—each individual creating heaven on Earth through a powerful internal connection of Love.

Your soul resides in Love, even when you are experiencing a moment of anger. Every experience is complete Love calling you to your empowerment.

Ascension can be an interesting process for those who enjoy the discovery of the "problems" of life as puzzle-like games. There will be periods of challenges and periods of integration that don't feel exciting or blissful. These are opportunities for new solutions and change. The process is easier to enjoy when you are clear about the outcome—an immersion in Love and the thrill of synchronicity abounding. That is when you really begin to hear Life speaking to you of Love—even in challenging situations. First, you must remove the blocks to hearing this music.

Light Language is one tool of clarity that can assist the process of Ascension through release and realization. The heart, the main component of Ascension, is the vehicle of connection, empathy, and release as you align with your glow of Love. The brain, the beautiful mechanism of understanding, is the path to realization. *The Ascended human has a symbiotic heart/mind balance that opens the full capacity of the body, the biomechanism, as a divine vehicle.* Light Language is one of the divine gifts that begins to flow through you. Not all want or need it, but it is one aspect of the open heart and mind that flows as loving communication of Spirit.

Your Ascension is guaranteed. It is not a "maybe." Humanity has crossed a threshold of uncertainty about the current path of Ascension, and as a soul you are eternal Love. Feel the power of your individual Love, and feel the power of the vast support of Love that All Life holds for you. Your soul resides in Love, even when you are experiencing a moment of anger or hatred.

Every experience is complete Love calling you to your empowerment. Light Language is a wonderful ally in this natural evolution.

Ascension is the thriving of Life on Earth.

It has begun.

It will continue.

Through you.

Chapter Twelve

Light Language and DNA

Deoxyribonucleic acid, or DNA, is the instructions that create and maintain your physical body. DNA stores genetic information used to create new cells or new organisms. Each cell in your body contains DNA, which is a string of physical information contained in about three billion base pairs comprised of chemical components. Imagine how small DNA must be to fit three billion chemical pairs into a single cell of your body. Yet, these base pairs form two incredibly long strands that spiral into a double helix shape when they stretch out for duplication. During normal cell operation, the DNA forms a torus, which is shaped like a doughnut.

Light Language and DNA | 143

This form is what allows information to flow so quickly, and for such vast information to be stored within such a small space, like a cell that is too small for our eyes to see.

Science has made great strides in studying the DNA, even working across country lines to map the human genome. However, beyond conventional science, there are promising experiments that are beginning to show that DNA does more than sequence chemical components. In part, it reads your emotions, your mental projections, and your beliefs. These are also part of the instruction sets that make up your building blocks. Your DNA reads and responds to the information you transmit to it, most of it unconscious.

> ***Your DNA is a vehicle of Light, for in its core processing functionality, it creates Light and responds to Light.***

Scientific experiments—though still technically just theory rather than accepted proof—have been able to determine some of the results of the unseen nature of DNA. For example, a Russian scientist named, Vladimir Poponin furthered the research of his colleague Peter Gariaev on the theory known as "The DNA Phantom Effect." In Poponin's experiments, DNA organized photons in a vacuum and the pattern remained even after the DNA was no longer present. This points to the quantum entanglement of DNA, that it can affect an environment when it is no longer present, creating a cohesion of information through sustained light organization. In my opinion, it also begins to blur the linearity of time and space.

There are nascent studies into the ability of DNA to respond and change based on words, just like Dr Emoto's work showed words and prayers affected the structure of water crystals. Words include thought and intent, with intent being the real catalyst, because it is the true meaning behind all verbal communication. From my personal experience, I believe the resonance of DNA is able to change based on intent.

Over a decade ago, my Guides showed me that each human's DNA is 0.0000000000000000001 percent different from another's. That is eighteen zeros after the decimal and before the one. In other words, all of our DNA is very similar. Yet look at how differently you perceive yourself to be from others: different genders, races, height, weight, intelligence, and more. I was told each person has characteristics and stories that define the self, but in reality the stories are all the same but for a 0.0000000000000000001 percent difference. Each story contains a different name, gender, location, and other details, but essentially it is the same story of birth, challenge, triumph, relief, or loss. This is yet another example of how connected you actually are to others, even as physical reality would seem to tell a different story.

DNA AND LIGHT

Your DNA responds to vibrational information. It is a vehicle of Light, for in its core processing functionality, it creates Light and responds to Light (as well as sound and intent). This is what I experience as I intuitively observe DNA. It relays information through the frequencies of Light, which can also be heard as sound or seen as color.

Light Language speaks directly to DNA. Light is a carrier of quantum frequency information. This frequency information is a catalyst for the chemical responses in your body. As Light Language communicates with your DNA, the frequency of Love (and the details of that information for you) adjust the resonance, or the instructions your DNA maintains. Perhaps the transmission communicates details of forgiveness for your parents, self-love for your perceived imperfections, or a new perspective of a lost love providing the gift of a new direction.

Much of the functionality of DNA is unknown. Humanity's scientific process is geared to learn from what is observable and repeatable. Beyond the repeatable is a spiritual aspect of humanity I believe is part of the interaction that can't be defined by protein coding alone. The unknown nature of DNA comprises volumes in and of itself, but suffice it to say that it is an interdimensional, conscious functionality of Life our current scientific instruments are unable to accurately and fully define. What was once considered "junk DNA" is now being understood as perhaps an unknown process, but scientists are starting to see that it is actually doing something. Nature does not maintain such a large percentage of extraneous physical structure through evolution. The DNA that is not responsible for physical coding is interdimensional in nature, but a bridge for your energetic information, such as your Akashic records, and your physical experience. For a continued study of the interdimensional aspects of DNA, *The Twelve Layers of DNA: An Esoteric Study of the Mastery Within*, by Lee Carroll is recommended reading.

INVISIBLE CONNECTION

Your physical system is a microcosm of a macrocosm. Physicists Nassim Haramein and Elizabeth Rauscher have mathematically theorized the fractal scale of interconnection.[1] This Universal Scaling Law is a profound step toward understanding the relationship between all aspects of life. Having evidence that there is a ratio of scale between a proton and our galaxy allows for a more tangible understanding of humanity's interconnection with the entire cosmos. It explains the fractal nature of the universe. This, in turn, helps individuals recognize their connection with the collective of humanity. The scientific correlation assists in releasing mental resistance that blocks humans from recognizing their invisible, connected nature.

The invisible aspect of life is far vaster than the visible. When channeling the Language of Light, one is tapping into the "invisible" field (space) and pulling through accessible information and transmitting it through visible and audible sound, shape, light and movement. The physical aspects of life, those that are discernable by the five senses, are the smallest parts

---

1 Haramein, N., Rauscher, E.A., and Hyson, M. (2008). Scale Unification: A Universal Scaling Law. Proceedings of the Unified Theories Conference. ISBN 9780967868776; http://resonance.is/explore/publications/.

of it. During a channeling (and prior to encountering the Universal Scaling Law), my nonphysical Guide Areon taught me that just as the atom is more than ninety-nine percent space and less than one percent matter, so too, are humans and All of Life. The physical body is only one small aspect of you; much of your self is in a faster (higher) vibrational frequency and therefore invisible to you.

The five physical senses of taste, touch, smell, sight and hearing each also have a higher-frequency sensory capability known as intuitive or psychic senses. These senses discern higher (or lower) vibrating, less physical information. There are other psychic senses that are not directly associated with the five physical senses, such as the ability to channel information from beings who do not reside in humanity's physical frequency spectrum.

I was taught that this ratio of ninety-nine percent space and one percent matter applies to other experiences, like ninety-nine percent invisible action (imagination, thoughts, feelings) and one percent visible action. An interesting one that came up directly is that your personal boundaries are ninety-nine percent invisible action (your boundaries are held by your beliefs, intent, and choices) and one percent visible action (saying no or confronting someone when needed).

Light Language is an informational frequency that works directly with your DNA.

This same ratio of ninety-nine percent space/invisible and one percent matter/visible applies to the Language of Light in the sense that much of the information is invisible to the physical senses; it resides in a frequency that cannot be easily deciphered and translated into a few human words. It contains volumes of information and healing frequencies within one percent of audible or written data.

DNA Activation

Many people refer to "DNA Activation" as opening to more of your nonphysical nature and activating latent DNA capabilities, or the instructions your body uses to maintain itself. One example is activating your DNA through meditation or energy healing; you may find your intuition has increased, or you have healing energy emanating from your hands.

The activation of your DNA is powerful for beginning to work with the subtle realms. There are many ways to activate or change your DNA; the mere act of forgiveness changes your DNA, as the information of resentment and anger you released through forgiveness was part of the instructions your DNA repeatedly replicated into your cells. This is why forgiveness is such a powerful tool—it is not the acceptance of someone else's bad behavior, it is the release of vibrational information (anger, disgust, sorrow, despair, victimhood, blame) that has been residing in you. Your new vibration contains more empowerment, compassion, discernment and Love. This allows for greater interaction with the higher realms of existence through your Light vehicle of DNA.

> *Light Language does not bypass your free will; it works directly with your pure intent.*

Any sort of evolution is a DNA Activation, because you begin to work more with your natural capacities that you weren't utilizing before. As a larger example, humanity did not undergo any physical changes to evolve into agrarian societies; it merely developed a new way of using something that was always available. When humans began utilizing agriculture, the experience of life changed dramatically. The same occurs with a DNA Activation. You begin to access what was always available before, but now that you are aware of and utilizing it, your life experience changes.

Just interacting with Light Language begins to activate your DNA into your discovery of new abilities as *it telepathically stimulates the loving, higher vibrating capacities of your brain and heart*. It changes your DNA bit by bit, moment by moment, as is appropriate for your growth. *Light Language is an informational frequency that works directly with your DNA*. The reason it is so effective with your DNA is that your mental constructs don't block your ability to change. *Light Language does not bypass your free will; it works directly with your pure intent.*

If you want improvement, but can't find forgiveness for something blocking you, Light Language will help you access that forgiveness through your Higher Self. Don't give up on yourself. Because humanity is learning personal empowerment as a species, some of the healing will be your conscious work, but it also occurs as your DNA responds to the Language of Light.

Chapter Thirteen

The Higher Self

Your Higher Self is the less-dense, nonphysical part of you. It is your direct connection with God and All Life. It is your direct connection with the full understanding of your innate divinity. Because of the word "higher," it is easy to think of your Higher Self as being separate from you and residing outside of you (perhaps up in heaven, out in space or only surrounding you like an aura). Since your Higher Self is not physical, it is not bound by time or space. It is in you, outside of you, and everywhere. It is the part of you that vibrates at a higher frequency. It is the vast, subtle, "ninety-nine percent space" part of you.

Your Higher Self is the connected nature of Self. It is fully connected to you and it relays information to your heart/mind complex and body. It is connected to All Life in full understanding and awareness, and maintains the connection of the "separate" you in physical form with your soul, soul group(s), and All That Is.

The Higher Self mimics the fractal nature of Life. It resides in the invisible realm of Love (connection); therefore, the earthly challenges humans perceive are viewed from a different perspective than what the Higher Self perceives and experiences. The Higher Self does not see a problem as permanent misfortune, but as an opportunity. It does not see you as ever making a mistake, but as a human experiencing, learning and progressing. It calls you repeatedly to your ability to give and receive Love, for it knows Love through and through. It knows you as Love in human form.

As you resolve your unconscious fears and resistance, new solution is a natural progression of your life.

Your Higher Self is the nonphysical part of you that is timeless, omniscient, and unconditionally Loving. Every experience you have in life is your Higher Self speaking to you of Love. Did you experience a triumph? This is a reminder of the Love you deserve so freely in your life. Did you experience a challenge? This is a reminder of the Love you deserve so freely in your life, but through the opposite point of attraction. Your Higher Self calls you to your empowerment, which ultimately allows you to create and

Love more freely. As you harmonize with your Higher Self, challenges become easier to navigate, and *when appropriate*, to circumnavigate.

COMMUNICATING WITH YOUR HIGHER SELF

You do not need to hear words spoken by your Higher Self, for it is always communicating with you. Because the Higher Self is you in subtle form, the communication may not seem so distinct from you. It speaks to you through your emotions, synchronicities, or dreams. It conveys data through your intuitive senses. It is constantly flowing information to you, so as you become more aware, you will find communication everywhere. It communicates to you through music, books, television, social media, advertisements, conversations with others, and much more. Your communication with your Higher Self may be subtle, but it is constant and unlimited.

Your Higher Self sets up experiences that show you what is in your subconscious mind. Ascension is a path of empowerment and Love. To become empowered, you find the blockages in your unconscious mind and choose a new focus—one of Love in its many facets. You are essentially becoming conscious of what is in your subconscious mind. This is the focus of my healing sessions: I assist clients in releasing the unconscious beliefs and traumas that interrupt the flow of empowerment and Love. You also do this by observing what occurs in your life.

Reading the clues of life becomes fun when you realize Life is conspiring for your improvement. The clues come from your Higher Self. Whether through a triumph or a challenge, your Higher Self is guiding you toward your improvement. In each moment, you have a choice as to how you will interact with your surroundings. As *you resolve unconscious fears and resistance, the evolution of new solution is a natural progression of life.* This is the core of creating your reality.

CREATING YOUR REALITY

Every experience in your life is magnetized to you by the vibration you emit. Your vibration is the sum total of all your thoughts, feelings, known beliefs, unknown beliefs, actions, intentions and to a lesser extent, your words. (A lesser extent because you can say words that don't match your true intent.) Therefore, as you read the clues of information in every experience you have, even of occurrences you hear about on the news, you become aware of what is in your subconscious mind.

Life merely responds to your vibration, and the experiences you have offer you the choice to change. Life is never punishing you; it is merely responding to vibration. Change is a constant in life, and your changes are a response to your choices. You can make conscious choices, or you can react out of habit. You can choose from insecurity or you can choose from empowerment and love. You have the power of choice in each moment.

Your awareness of the subconscious programming that creates unwanted experiences in your life helps you make choices from a place of empowerment. The Higher Self, the nonphysical part of you is always showing you how to progress into an empowered, sovereign, Loving person. It merely requires your astute attention to discern the communication, as well as your courage to choose anew. Every experience calls you to your empowerment. Your Higher Self never loses sight of the Love you are and the potential growth contained in each moment.

The focus of the Higher Self is your *Soul Progression*. The Higher Self is merely the part of you that understands life from a broader perspective. This broader perspective is the timeless, omniscient, unconditionally loving part of self. It is your God-like nature and the reason it has been stated that humans are made in God's image. God's "image" is timeless, omniscient, and unconditionally Loving. This also points to the power of *imag*ination.

Light Language is a profound communication with your Higher Self; your Higher Self speaks it fluently.

As humans, we bring Source perspective to Earth in human form. An animal brings that energy in animal form, a plant brings it in plant form, and a rock brings it in rock form. As you exist on Earth, you forget the divinity you are, it becomes unconscious. Your earthly existence is a construct of the physical density and dimensional structures that define separation in physicality. The forgetting is a necessary part of the remembering.

Soul Progression for Ascension

Ascension is the process of aligning your Higher Self with your human self as you elevate your physical vibrational frequency to include a broader spectrum of nonphysical experience. As you do this, you become connected to a fuller experience of life, more in alignment with your creative divinity.

Ascension is a development of your conscious, Loving empowerment through connection with the Higher Self—connection beyond the visible moment. It is connection beyond audible words, into the inaudible yet potently creative intent. Ascension leads you to craft a life attuned to your greatest purpose—enjoying being human.

Light Language is a profound communication with your Higher Self; your Higher Self speaks it fluently. The Languages that come through you (or that you are drawn to receive) are a reflection of your soul's history and your life path on Earth. Your Higher Self transduces the frequencies so they are healing and expansive at the appropriate pace for you. As you communicate more deeply with and through your Higher Self, you expand your physical experience to integrate a higher vibration of Love and connection, which is the resonance of Light Language.

Chapter Fourteen

The Heart

The heart is the first physical organ to form in a human fetus. But what about the esoteric heart of a human—the spirit of love and connection? I believe it weaves into the physical functionality of the heart. The heart circulates blood around the physical body with an internally generated electronic pulse that contracts the muscles and pushes blood throughout the body system, nourishing it and sustaining it. Esoterically, the heart is the functionality that connects you with the system of Life.

The energy of the heart is the energy of emotions. Emotions are a connective force. They entwine you with a deep understanding, empathy, and perspective of All Life. Your emotions are indicators of information, as they contain vast amounts of data within succinct categories. Most importantly, they indicate to you what information is within your own energy field—often what resides in your unconscious mind. *Allowing healthy emotional flow is commensurate with allowing learning and healing to occur.*

Every cell and organ emits an electromagnetic field. The heart has the strongest electromagnetic field of the body, much greater than the second strongest electromagnetic field of the brain. Humans are still rather brain-centric, valuing statistical data and cunning over healthy emotional flow and compassionate commerce. This has and will change over time as people begin to heal the fears that polarize them toward domination and deception.

Your Emotional Signals

Emotions are information along a wide spectrum of experience. To say you are "happy" can mean many different things. It could mean extreme excitement, satisfaction, calm, or many other variances of happiness. Your body system naturally correlates similar experiences and categorizes them for data retrieval when necessary. This is a vital functionality of the brain/body complex that eases your interaction with life; it is also a functionality of learning.

As you observe and heal your emotional imbalances (avoidance and repression of unhealed trauma), you will find that progress and wisdom become available. Emotions help to reveal your innate empowerment of creative interplay with Life. The entire spectrum of emotions is a valuable aspect of human life. As you heal your emotional imbalances, you create a balanced power in your internal world, where choice resides. *When you are balanced in your flow of emotions, you are able to choose rather than react.*

THE EMOTIONS OF ASCENSION

The path of Ascension entails coming into balance with energy, or integrating it into wholeness, before expanding beyond it. Therefore, coming to terms with the symptoms and systems that polarize people into destructive actions must balance before they can be moved beyond. You do this first in your internal world, then your external world. That change ripples out beyond you through choice. Much of my private session work and classes are about teaching people to deal with the mental and emotional aspects of Ascension. As every individual makes new and better choices, life improves for all.

> ***When you are balanced in your flow of emotions, you are able to choose rather than react.***

Choice is the vehicle of empowerment and Love. As you heal the issues that keep you stuck in unhealthy patterns of thoughts and actions, you begin to interact with everything from a more balanced, stable energy. This has a profound impact on you and a relative impact on all sovereign beings you interact with or who experience the same issues. Each person has the free will choice to change or not change. However, as you heal your own emotional issues, you change how you interact with others and how they interact with you. Relationships are no longer controlled or feared. Your creativity is not resisted, nor is the mundane.

For example, paying your taxes may not bring you joy, but you can choose to release money to your government for the services it provides without anger or fear of lack. It merely requires the empowerment of knowing you are capable of creating within restrictive or negative-feeling systems. This is where your freedom is. You benefit from your energetic flow of ease and knowing your power to remain balanced. You are shifting government systems for the better as you interact with them with the easy flow of less resistance, more appreciation, and trust that all is well and improving. This is invisible, yet potent. Few people truly know the power of their vibrational interactions because the results are not immediately obvious. Therefore, the potential influence of these experiences is weakened because it is not amplified by intent. *The intent of the heart, the strongest electromagnetic field of your system, is a mighty catalyst.*

Resolving Emotional Imbalance

Balancing the energy of the heart means coming into a state of connection with Life where your energy flows easily, without resistance. "Good" or "bad" does not throw you off-balance when you are in this easy flow with Life—at least not as much or not for as long. As you repel from or rail against what feels bad and seek only what feels good, you do not have the power of a balanced, empowered state of connection with Life.

Your power resides within your capability to observe and interact with life while maintaining the strength of your own balance. This means your emotions flow rather than remain a monotone of peace or joy that is actually based on avoidance of challenging feelings like sadness, anger or fear. Authenticity with how you genuinely feel in the moment is necessary to get to this place of balance.

If you hate someone or something, feel it with the intent of healing your hatred and your body system will naturally begin to release the emotion in helpful ways. You may need to take some healthy action steps, like yelling at a wall, listening to fast music, dancing, crying, or venting to an empowering friend. You may not feel bliss immediately, but you are beginning a valuable healing process. Avoiding the challenging feeling keeps it within you, suppressed to surface in another way. Healing it brings new solutions and possibilities into your life. A "negative" emotion is merely an indicator of an energy imbalance. It calls you to your empowerment and full flow with Life.

The intent of the heart, the strongest electromagnetic field of your system, is a mighty catalyst.

When humans avoid emotions, they separate from the full integration of Self with Life. They remain disempowered in dealing with life. Being authentic with your emotions is different from spewing them indiscriminately. Quite often people interact from their insecurities because their conscious minds are unaware of how to integrate empowerment. They unconsciously interact from the survival fears of needing to be valuable or needing attention; tribal fears that relate to survival.

Survival fears go well beyond feeding the body or keeping it warm. For example, survival fears in the workplace manifest as hiding incompetence, slandering others, stealing ideas, manipulating, or lying. Survival fears in relationships result in putting your loved ones down or harming them physically, verbally or emotionally. The marketing engine uses various mechanisms to manipulate people's survival fears.

Healthy emotional flow begins by observing what you are authentically feeling with as much detachment as possible in the moment. If detachment isn't readily available to you, wait until you are calm enough to observe yourself more objectively. This is the reason people practice taking ten breaths before responding with anger—it helps you gain some perspective before reacting.

Neutral Observance

Detached observation allows you to find internal information about a fear or lack that is leading to a negative emotional reaction. This is the equivalent of being loving with yourself and others during a challenge. It doesn't mean you don't care. It means you care enough not to get pulled off-balance by drama or fear. Your neutrality helps you remain centered and grounded during challenging situations.

Negative emotions are not bad. They are wonderful indicators of the Love and empowerment that is lacking in your psyche, which affects your choices. How you deal with negative emotions is key to your empowered interaction with life. As you observe your feelings with detachment, you start an energetic dialogue with your subconscious mind. This signals a level of awareness that supports the release of imbalanced emotions. This release can be healthy, and even interesting, when you maintain a neutral focus.

In the moment you recognize that you hate your boss and wish he or she would get fired and then die a horrible death, you feel bad. The emotion itself is uncomfortable. Then you realize you also feel guilty for having the feeling, angry at life for the situation, hopeless to be able to resolve it, and many other emotions.

The situation can become a quagmire of negative emotions and disempowerment. What you might do—because of survival fears—with sufficient time and distraction is suppress the emotion. You may keep out of the boss's way as much as possible or take verbal and emotional abuse quietly and wait for the emotion to fester and manifest into a different problem that may not have an obvious connection to this situation.

When you are neutral enough to access a balanced emotional state, you can begin to pursue new solutions from a place of empowerment rather than fear.

There is so much data on diseases that are related to stress (as one example), that the emotional and mental connection to your physical health is no longer a theory, it is a medical fact.

Not every health problem is caused by an emotional blockage; however, emotional blockage always leads to depleted or detrimental physical and mental health. Not just in the obvious ways, such as feeling depressed and eating badly or not exercising, but also in the energetics of your holistic flow. It is a serious problem humanity is in the nascent stages of recognizing and rectifying. Begin with yourself.

Recognize the first stages of disappointment, then speak of them or write about them with the intention of healing them. For example, if you've been unexpectedly fired from a job, your first reaction might be anger. That anger might create an urge to cry, worry, or numb the fear of, "What's next?" Take some action steps to help that energy transform from anger and fear into new possibilities. Take a walk, a run, use Light Language to surface blockages or talk to a supportive friend. These are just a few ways of dealing with that uncomfortable energy.

When you are neutral *enough* to access a balanced emotional state, you can begin to pursue new solutions from a place of empowerment rather than fear. The answer to, "What's next?" is easier than you've been led to believe. You are powerful and you are connected to your Higher Self, which knows the deep Love of Life and the potentials available from what seems like a bad situation. Get calm enough to access a meditative state and receive the energy of your Higher Self.

You were drawn to this book because you are capable of becoming empowered, even if you need assistance to attain it. Empowerment is a lifelong and worthy pursuit. It is a topic I have been teaching for many years because it is essential for healing. Not only does it change your life for the better, it changes the world.

Healing Emotions

Practice observing your emotions with a neutrality that also knows deeply that feeling authentic emotions is healthy, spiritual, and safe. Emotions are meant to flow in healthy ways, even though they don't always feel good in the moment. As you feel and observe your negative emotions, remind yourself that as you feel them you are healing them. *You are resolving the feeling into a lesson learned as you honor its existence.* Why? Because as you honor a negative emotion, you access its opposite—a positive emotion.

Releasing hatred resolves it into empowered observance of behaviors you are choosing not to emulate. Releasing anger resolves it into empowered boundaries of self-love. Releasing sorrow resolves it into the creativity of flowing with life, letting go, and opening to the new. Be patient and diligent, as not everything heals in a nanosecond, and some situations also require action, such as talking with your boss, leaving an unhealthy relationship or holding a boundary.

You do not need to immerse yourself in negative emotions. You are served by honoring them into resolution when they are present. When you feel so angry at your boss that you desire revenge, your work isn't to wallow there, it is to honor that you feel angry, helpless, and hopeless. Honor the flow of space and time as you allow those feelings to transform into a new strength growing within you. Give the pain to God, that greater energy where the wisdom of the universe resides, to heal. You are an aspect of that wisdom, and Life wants you to thrive. You are Life in human form.

Creating with Emotions

When people first learn that they create their reality with the focus of their thoughts and feelings, it is exhilarating; they assume, for example, they can think positive thoughts about a new car and it will manifest. Then they realize they have many negative thoughts, and this scares them into creative shutdown. They observe that some people with harmful intentions create massive wealth and power. On the personal level, they may have tried to influence better behavior in someone they knew to be difficult, but that person's behavior did not change.

This becomes confusing and defeating. They must assume that either they are a failure at manifesting their reality, or what they thought was true was actually a lie—which leads to even more disempowerment and lack of trust in the self and the process of Life.

> ***When others deplete your energy, it is an indicator of survival fears leading your choices.***

It is frustrating for people not to have a specific mathematical formula for manifestation like the scientific method of repeatability. You do not get to decide how many positive thoughts you need to think about your boss for your desired manifestation of change to happen. You do not get to decide the exact outcome of a situation. You must also take action in life; it is not *just* about thinking and feeling.

Do the work of observing your emotions and thoughts until you see manifestation. It begins with your inner experience of more peace, then it begins to manifest in the external experiences of your life. You have to continue observing and improving your emotions and thoughts until manifestation is maintained consistently. You will notice you are not thrown off-balance by others and you feel peaceful joy on a more regular basis. Once you reach this new setpoint of stability, you are on an exciting, rewarding, and life-long journey of self-discovery and empowerment.

EMPOWERED LOVE

Your heart is a powerful gateway to your personal freedom. As you learn to feel your emotions and move through them in healthy ways, you open yourself to creative flow and enjoyment of Life. Hold the empowered boundaries that serve your choices and your open flow to experience Life—even the challenging moments. You will find over time that what once challenged you is now easier, or not a challenge at all.

An open heart does not allow others to deplete your life force. *On the contrary, when others deplete your energy, it is an indicator of survival fears leading your choices.* As appropriate, say no with the Love that teaches you and others that each person is a sovereign, loving being who learns empowerment through discovering individual inner strength. Sometimes that includes reaching out for assistance or assisting another, but continued personal depletion is not healthy for anyone involved.

As an example, an empowered mother will say yes to feeding her hungry baby, even when she would rather rest, because the situation calls for compromise and giving. An empowered mother may say no to feeding her hungry teenager while she rests, as the teenager is perfectly capable of feeding him or herself in that moment. That is an example of an empowered boundary in action, specific to the situation, and ultimately benefiting all involved.

LANGUAGE OF THE HEART

Light Language is an effective tool for dealing with emotions, as it works deeply with the heart. *It is a catalyst of release and resolution that bypasses your mental constructs and speaks directly to your heart.* That means it deals with your connective, supportive energy with Life. For instance, it goes beyond your need to mentally figure out how to resolve the situation with your boss and convince him or her to treat you with respect. It heals the wounds within you that are magnetizing the experience to you. Even if you still need to take the action of standing up for yourself, Light Language can help to ease that process. Each situation is unique.

> *Light Language bypasses your mental constructs and speaks directly to your heart.*

As you utilize the Language of Light for healing, you will find a greater foundation of peace growing in your life. Peace is a state of neutrality and openness that supports you with great balance. As you observe the quick, decisive actions of paramedics responding to an accident, notice how they are exemplifying a variance of peace. It certainly does not look the same as a meditative state, but it is along the spectrum of peace. A trained paramedic does not get thrown off-balance by the trauma of an accident. Paramedics maintain detachment and focus so they can interact with challenging situations with wisdom rather than fear.

As you reveal your empowerment to yourself and really begin to live your life fully, you will be pleasantly surprised at what you find within. You are truly a treasure waiting to be unburied and enjoyed. You are the beautiful jewel of Life. As you live this truth, you show others they are beautiful as well. Your heart is the treasure of your chest, for it is the sweetness of your connection with Life pulsing within you.

Chapter Fifteen

The Brain

Life on Earth is a holographic expression interpreted and materialized by humans' physical sensory capacities. Your entire biomechanism is a sensory machine that is continuously receiving, interpreting and emitting vibrational data. From your conscious perspective, the brain interprets sensory data, sends signals, and then you have an experience. But that is only one small part of the equation, as the heart is the connective instrument and the brain is the analyzer and linearizer of the information the heart receives and emits. Additionally, the heart/mind complex is only one part of your full body mechanism that connects you with Life.

The brain categorizes, analyzes, compares, and deconstructs data. Then the brain connects data. These abilities are valuable. No mistake was made when the brain was created. It has within its makeup the capability to progress toward empowerment, which many see as its failing when they observe imbalanced ego. The brain can be fooled, ignored, distracted or emphasized; all of which lead to its downfall of rigid, limited belief structures and lack of expansion.

> **As the brain is empowered into an open state, a connection with the ever-present, unseen, higher-frequency, subtle dimensions is attained.**

This points to the importance of empowerment; each valuable individual has the capability to focus his or her brain onto its highest path. The neural paths worn by habit or avoidance (two similar, though distinct, energies) are changed by choice. The Language of Light helps you shift these neural pathways, but conscious choice is the most powerful vehicle of change. It is said that one reason the Pentecostals are often depicted with fire above their head is because as they spoke in Light Language the neural nodes "fired" more distinctly and activated the higher chakras.

The human brain and mind/body system can evolve into a broader spectrum of information interpretation that expands the individual into greater interaction with Life. It is a powerful catalyst for this evolution as it activates higher-functioning capabilities that are inherent to the brain, but not generally active or used. *The Book of Knowledge: The Keys of Enoch* by Dr. J.J. Hurtak points out that Light Language creates "instant Communication with the Infinite Mind to code knowledge. This allows man to have communion with other planets of intelligence through super-holographic processes." Light Language expands the brain's natural capacities.

The brain interprets dimensional rules, limitations and the functionality of the dimensional playing field. As the brain is empowered into an open state, a connection with the ever-present, unseen, higher-frequency, subtle dimensions is attained. This is accomplished by leading with the heart and following that information with the magnificent defining, refining, and reforming capabilities of the brain.

Valuable Data

The brain works by interpreting vibrational data into a format the senses can extract, define and utilize. Just as a computer can create images and functions from zeros and ones, your brain creates experience from frequency. For instance, the vibrational frequencies of a walk in nature are received as the smell of flowers, the sound of birds, the sound and feel of wind, or the sight of light shining through leaves. It also includes tactile sensations like rocks and the bark of trees (you know you want to hug them!), temperature, barometric pressures, and much more. The brain translates a vast amount of information from vibration into sensory data. The data does not stop being vibrational, but as the brain transposes it, it becomes a smell or a sound to your senses.

> **The brain translates a vast amount of information from vibration into sensory data. The data does not stop being vibrational, but as the brain transposes it, it becomes a smell or a sound to your senses.**

The brain is only able to interpret what it is exposed to, and must gradually learn to move beyond receiving into understanding. Learning is a lifetime pursuit. It is highly active during childhood, moving through different degrees of subconscious focus into conscious focus.

In a young child, the subconscious mind is dominant; data is easily received but not consciously interpreted. The vibrational frequencies of the people and situations around the child are recorded into the brain. As the child grows, the conscious mind gradually becomes more active. In the teen years, the frontal lobe becomes more developed, allowing for more conscious choice rather than subconscious imprinting. In the adult years, the option of melding the conscious and subconscious mind is more fully available, as the control of the parents is surpassed.

Many adults stop learning into the depth of the subconscious and just live in habitual thought and action. This is why it is important to seek out continued learning, spiritual growth, new experiences and to become accustomed to change as you make new choices in your life. Evolution is a process of conscious awareness of your inner motivations (they are often subconscious until you observe them) and external choices.

Ascension is the path of continuing to learn, or evolve, into an elevated human who utilizes the conscious and subconscious brain in order to expand the connection with the invisible life around him or her. The energy of Love connects, and Love is invisible. The information of the subconscious mind is invisible until it is brought forth into the light of awareness. Light Language is one such vehicle connecting the brain and the heart.

Expanding the Mind

The brain opens doorways when it meets with certain frequencies. For example, a smell or a song can open a doorway into the subconscious as it triggers memories. Light Language works in a similar way, as it speaks to the subconscious mind directly, helping humans access what is held within, but as yet unknown. The Language of Light helps teach the brain by triggering the release of misinformation that is contrary to the truth of Love.

As you interact with the Language of Light, you expand how your brain deals with language.

The mental construct often blocks new information as the neural pathways are challenged. In psychology this is called cognitive dissonance. We could also call this an ego groove or a habit pathway. It is a belief structure that has served the person's progress and now that person is being pressed into expansion. A feeling of resistance is a sign you are recognizing a limitation that you must push past. This is why Light Language can be so effective; it speaks directly to the subconscious mind so the resistance melts away from within. This is also why people tend to cry when they hear it—the heart is dissolving and releasing resistance.

Whether you are receiving or transmitting Light Language, you are utilizing the conceptual right-brain functionality. When you are translating the meaning of a Light Language transmission, you are using the left-brain functionality. However, to merely separate the left and right brain is not the whole picture, but Light Language supports the two hemispheres of the brain working together. *As you interact with the Language of Light, you expand how your brain deals with language, because you are not utilizing the normal speech centers.* It is the beginning of telepathic/empathic communication. Eventually humanity will learn to understand the full extent of Light Language and all other communication on deeper levels.

Your Brain, Your Choice

The brain is a beautiful and perfect mechanism for the progression of Life. The ego structure is also. Progress is not forced; it is found. Circumstances do not create or block progress, for humans can make an internal choice about how to react and respond to any situation. This is why choice is so vital—freedom really comes from within.

> ***Light Language is a powerful catalyst of heart/mind communication.***

No one can force you to think a thought, but you can allow yourself to be coerced. Ascension entails humanity moving into greater consciousness as we each become more aware of the unseen mechanisms that propel Life. This is an advanced brain functionality humanity must embody in order to evolve. As you become more aware, you become more actively creative. As the brain expands its functionality, the heart becomes less limited.

It is within the power of the brain to ask why, and it is within the power of the ego to desire the best for the self. However, since many humans are not taught to self-reflect and self-nurture, many circle in dysfunction without understanding how they can find solution.

> ***The Language of Light stretches the brain into communicating with data that is beyond learned words.***

Life is always a balance of the inner and the outer, of receiving and giving. Clues to the answers you seek are often outside of you, but the final decision is within you—you have the power of choice. The brain and the ego help discern what choices best suit your current path. When those wonderful mechanisms of discernment and choice follow the open heart, empowerment is attained. It is the natural progression of Life, and these mechanisms are perfect and brilliant when utilized fully and properly.

The Language of Light stretches the brain into communicating with data that is beyond learned words. It functions as a bridge for full-body communication because the vibration does not get blocked by mental constraints of what is true (known fact) or believed to be possible. It begins to open telepathic channels by expanding the brain's ability to extract understanding from non-linear information. The human expands into healing, understanding and connection with a broader range of abilities and information.

Light Language is a powerful catalyst of heart/mind communication. It expands the understanding of the depth of information communicated beyond audible words. It is opening brain capacity that is already there, but not usually consciously utilized as humanity only consciously uses a small portion of the natural capability of the brain. The Language of Light stretches individuals into personal discernment, choice, and an openness to the unknown becoming known through higher intelligence. Light Language is an experience of the brain expanding into the Divine mind.

Chapter Sixteen

The Ego

The ego and the brain both get a bad rap. They are merely mechanisms of understanding and survival that should be embraced and continually improved. To observe how your brain and ego cooperate with your spirit is the work of Ascension. It requires neutralizing into integration and expansion, which increases your vibrational frequency, aligns you with empowered Love and affects the world around you. Light Language assists this integration with frequencies of remembrance and application into new experiences such as the merging of time—past, present and future.

The ego is the way the brain identifies the self. It is the vehicle of individuality inherent to sentient life on Earth. Individuality is one part of life, as all individuality exists within a larger group. All Life is connected and not truly separate, though it is experienced as separate in this reality. This paradox is woven throughout life. We have an ego structure merely to continue life. Obliterating or resisting your ego is counterproductive. Balancing it so it doesn't stagnate your growth is productive.

Life is an efficient engine. Energy is never wasted or stopped; it merely entrains and transforms. Death is the same. Nothing dies and is gone forever; it transforms. For instance, when you eat a vegetable or an animal you are consuming life force. You are consuming vibration that has a certain energy. Your body takes this energy and creates various chemical combinations for your survival. But what of the vegetable or animal? Its life force is entraining with yours, weaving into your current chemicals and transforming from plant or animal into your human experience. Its vibrational information continues by entraining into your life force, even to the point of excretion, where it transforms into fertilizer that grows new life. This is the system of Life. It is all benevolent, even the ego. Every experience becomes fertilizer for new growth.

THE BENEFICIAL EGO

Your sweet ego is doing its best to keep you alive with whatever information it has to work with. For example, a firefighter with a balanced ego is effective during a forest fire, because he or she would keep a safe distance while actively trying to put the fire out. If that firefighter had no understanding of the power of the self (too little ego), the fire would continue to ravage until it stopped on its own. That firefighter would have to keep running farther away from the fire just to stay alive. Luckily, we have unconscious survival skills that compel us to do that when necessary. This firefighter has too little understanding of the power of the self, the imbalanced ego is blocking a better choice.

If the firefighter had an overinflated perspective of the power of the self (too much ego), he or she might endanger life. With blatant disregard for the power of the fire, the firefighter would likely get badly burned. With a feeling of superiority, the firefighter would not honor the power of forces (such as other firefighters or the power of the fire) outside of the self.

These two extremes may look like opposites, but they both stem from an imbalanced understanding of the power of the self *and* everything outside of the self.

A balanced ego structure honors the self as the life it is, and honors others for their innate power, too. *This gradual understanding results in moving from competition to cooperation and co-creation.* The unification of honoring the self and others is not the rejection of the ego or the self. Just as the individual organs in the body work together collectively to create the whole organism, your ego does, too.

As you embrace your individuality and find your internal balance, your ego expands its connection from identification of self to identification of self within the whole.

Your ego, whether in balance or out of balance, is merely a moment of experience. In order for Ascension or expansion to occur, the ego must become a little imbalanced (cognitive dissonance) to find its new expanded balance, just as you shift your physical body's balance to take a step forward. It doesn't always have to be a challenging or dramatic process, but it is a process of change. Changing the self is the work of Ascension. And change is constant!

The ego and the brain are mechanisms of understanding so the heart can continue to expand into more love, into more connection. As you expand into more love, your ego receives new information and new choices become available. *As you embrace your individuality and find your internal balance, your ego expands its connection from identification of self to identification of self within the whole.* It then begins to identify with the whole that contains the self. This healthy process results in an easier flow within the natural mechanism of growth: imbalance to new balance.

Balancing the Ego

Humans have a tendency to set goals and then focus on how those goals have not yet been met. In balance, this can be the beginning of the discovery of how you move toward goals. However, when the ego is fraught with fear and lack, derision is born. This is a result of the ego not being taught to self-reflect and self-nurture. You are perfect just as you are now, and you are always changing and expanding for your highest good.

Humans are generally taught to focus on how the self is imperfect and that they must strive to reach perfection. Given all the outside opposing information, perfection is impossible to achieve by human standards. It is inherently achieved by divine standards. As you shift your focus to the joy of expansion, the fun of learning, and the perfection of your individual path; you become balanced in the constant change of growth. Your balanced ego is a vital part of this process.

To balance your ego, self-reflection is necessary and it should be an interesting process. It may not always be a pleasant process, for it sometimes exposes hidden, uncomfortable feelings. That can be fascinating, however, when you remember the result is your improvement. From this loving and detached perspective, you know the end result is peace, ease and increased flow with Life that feels creative and manageable. The balanced ego is a strong container that expands with the Self, resulting in open, empowered change.

To balance your ego, self-reflection is necessary and it should be an interesting process.

As the ego and brain work together to observe the experiences of the self, each person becomes empowered and joyful, for they are able to connect with their hearts. Joyful and empowered people create a community of that same open, transforming energy. That community then creates systems of communication, education, governance and cooperation that support and sustain the whole community in new and better ways. That interconnected community becomes a state, a country, a continent, a world. Though it may not seem obvious now, humanity is ascending into this state of being.

Embracing Change

As you look within at your individual passions, like painting, sports, nature or teaching children; begin to self-reflect and ask yourself questions. "Why do I love this?" "What does it feel like when I feel successful or feel challenged with it?" "What do I receive from these projects?" These questions begin an internal answering process that will show you where your ego is balanced and imbalanced. When the answers feel peaceful and joyful, your ego is balanced and you are being true to yourself and your joy. When the answers feel desperate, unattainable, uneasy, guilty, competitive, or filled with uncomfortable feelings—your ego is imbalanced.

As you accept that you have an uncomfortable feeling, honor it and acknowledge it—even in its unknown or undefined state. You have opened a doorway to your subconscious mind for healing to begin. Your brain will then do its work, which is to follow the impulse of your heart, or your true intent. When you ask these questions with the intent of growth, growth is the result. When you ask with the intent of manipulation, manipulation is the result. Your heart always wants Love. As you honor an uncomfortable feeling, you allow your heart to love it into the Light of healing.

Light Language can be an effective tool to begin this process of opening and ego balancing. The opening is always within you through your choice, your intent. Because the Language of Light unfolds information through your Higher Self, you are releasing blocks that keep your ego from accessing the healing power of Divine Love. Love, the inherent information of Light Language, is a powerful instrument for your Ascension, and thus the Ascension of humanity.

As you balance your ego into a strong, flexible structure of support, you bring powerful change to the world through all your interactions. Your courage is greatly rewarded as you become stronger within and more capable of emanating and creating your intent with clarity.

Chapter Seventeen

Intent

You are energy. Your energy has a unique vibration in any given moment. Your vibration emanates out from you, as energy is always in motion. *Intent is the full information of your vibrational emanation.* It is the full information the engine of Life receives from you and responds to with immense and efficient unconditional Love.

Your intent is your core of creation. It is the reason the Placebo Effect skews medical statistics. As the prefix "in" implies, your intent is within you. You have many different layers of intent, even within a single interaction. *The work of becoming empowered is discovering your intent and refining it for your progress toward becoming a loving, powerful and creative human being.*

When you think a thought or speak a sentence, your intent comprises the additional information that may not be formed into conscious thought or word. Your intent may be counterpoint to your words or it may be congruent. *Light Language speaks directly to your intent, unearthing the core of your vibration that needs to be healed for your clarity or accessed for your empowerment.*

Intent is the frequency or the full information of your electromagnetic emanation. You emit frequencies at all times, just as you receive and interpret them. You are ensconced in myriad frequencies that your body interprets, though much of that is beyond your conscious mind. *Often it interprets from past pain until you heal from within.* For example, if a child grew up with a parent who often had irrational outbursts of anger, that child may become an adult who interacts with others with the intent of pleasing people, so as not to anger them. He or she may walk on eggshells as an adult because the intent not to cause anger in others is so strong, even though it is unconscious.

Light Language speaks directly to your intent, unearthing the core of your vibration that needs to be healed for your empowerment.

Your eyes interpret waves of light only within a certain frequency band. There are other frequencies of light around you, though you do not see them. In this same way, intent has the ability to be interpreted by some, but not all (those with eyes to see). Even personal intent can be unknown to the one emitting it, although a balanced ego clarifies this process. Your intent; however, radiates from you and creates a response from the people around you, even though much of this is unconscious. As you become more astute at interpreting your unspoken intent and the intent of those around you, you will be equipped to refine your intent.

The Courage to Look Within

Defining and refining your intent is an important aspect of creating your life and interacting with life from a balanced and empowered state. When you emit unidentified intents such as, "I feel incapable at my job," you unconsciously enact sabotaging behaviors. Others around you receive the vibrational information of your intent and respond in ways that may be unconscious even to them, yet your intent creates an experience that results in your incapability at the job. Humans have lost much of the ability to understand why life manifests as it does, and consequently feel powerless to outer circumstances. They come to a logical, though incomplete, assumption that life is happening to them.

In order to initiate change in your vibrational signal (intent), you must observe yourself and the response you receive from the outer world. This will help you determine what is within you that you would like to improve and change. It takes courage to admit and deal with negative feelings in healthy ways. The process can be uncomfortable at first. It is the beginning of bringing subconscious or suppressed intent to your consciousness for your empowered choice.

Remember, the ego system is set up for your survival. What is currently in your energy field is working for the ego; you are alive, so the ego has a vested interest in continuing the status quo. The lack of self-esteem in the hearts of so many people in this world is the reason there is so much resistance and fear of change. The lack of developed discernment and creative skills is the reason minds are not as nimble as they could be. This is changing; evolution is inevitable, though society would advance faster with concentrated effort on increasing individual emotional intelligence. However, the pace is perfect for now, because it allows for deep change and understanding to occur.

Your authenticity is the real catalyst for improvement.

Choice contains your true intent, so while you may choose to say yes when you want to say no, your choice to say yes contains the vibrational information of your true desire to say no. This means it also may have the energy of resentment, martyrdom, burden, or the belief that "life is sacrifice" contained within it. That same choice may well contain loving duty, opening to new experiences, or wisdom of the future benefit. It is a matter of discerning the true emotional intent behind choice.

Intent does not have to be perfectly loving at all times. Authenticity is the real catalyst for improvement. When you are authentic, you are able to observe and choose with regard to any intent that is not serving your highest good. This is the power of learning to discern and choose from a place of balance rather than fear.

Recognizing Intent

When someone says, "I love you," there are vast amounts of intent behind the words. The words are a recognized, audible, and therefore obvious, carrier vehicle. Often, the words are so solid to the listener that the intent is ignored. *This is why the evolution of humanity must include observing beyond the obvious and into the subtle realms—where intent resides.* The following are examples of some intentions that might be behind the words "I love you:"

- I respect and honor you
- I feel good when I think of you
- You remind me of what Love is
- I am attracted to you
- You inspire passion in me
- I hope you know how special you are
- I am blessed that you are in my life
- I need attention to amplify my life force
- I want sexual gratification
- I need loyalty to feel my worth
- I am afraid of being alone
- I only feel alive with extreme emotions
- If I can control you, I will feel powerful

- I feel my worth through you
- If you are not focused on me, I will feel great pain

These are just a few examples of intentions that could be behind those words. An infinite list of conscious and unconscious information can hide behind each thought, word and choice made by an individual. To connect with the full potential of the brain, each individual must release the chemical dependencies from unconscious emotional pain that block the brain's capability to function at a higher-frequency level. The need for attention, for example, is ultimately a chemical dependency. Habits of drugs or alcohol are obvious dependencies. The rigid ego structure of too much control and domination or too much submission are the proverbial elephants in the room.

As you observe your own emotional responses, you learn to utilize a swift response system. Your emotions contain volumes of information. Realizing you feel angry is a valuable book of information that need only be understood to the extent that you comprehend the pertinent data. You need not identify every similar experience of anger you've ever had—just enough to understand the basis for your feeling so you can identify it and choose a preferred intent. Anger always points to an internal feeling of powerlessness that is being brought to the conscious mind through an experience.

For example, if you feel incapable at your job, you will unconsciously enact behaviors that seem to be masking that feeling, but that are actually perpetuating it. You could have trouble saying no when asked to take on additional projects because you fear your negative response will make you appear incapable of handling your job. You may then become overwhelmed with duties and miss deadlines or sacrifice quality. You could have trouble asking for assistance in order to appear stronger than you feel. Some of your co-workers might unconsciously respond to your vibrational emanation and complete a task for you without being asked. Rather than being grateful for assistance, you might have a defensive fear response to avoid the invisible feeling of incapability. A typical fear response would be to find fault rather than graciously accepting help.

Light Language is a powerful healing tool for working with your intent, both conscious and unconscious.

These patterns of unconscious behavior escalate an environment of fear because no one is sure about how their actions or vulnerabilities will be received. Each person is constantly guessing about external motives and potential responses, since few are able to articulate the reality of their internal motives and emotions in a calm and healthy manner. It perpetuates lack of healthy communication and confusing rules of engagement.

HEALTHY INTENT

On the path of Ascension, you recognize healthy intent because it creates win-win situations. As you become clear with your intent, you will notice the alignment of energies responding to you. You will begin to discern when there is a dissonant vibrational emanation within you, such as "I want_____, but I feel undeserving." You will become adept at honoring the contrasting vibration you want to shift and your mere focus on release and realignment will begin the clearing process of your vibration.

> *On the path of Ascension, you recognize healthy intent because it creates win-win situations.*

Light Language is a powerful healing tool for working with your intent, both conscious and unconscious. Because it works so deeply with the heart, it is a catalyst for the release of much of what has been blocked. It opens new avenues of empowerment from within, in alignment with the Higher Self's choice of the person receiving it. Light Language begins the healing process of imbalanced, often unconscious, fear and trauma. It stirs new choices into experiences and supports empowerment growing through the wisdom of the being. This changes the energetic structure so that the constant and invisible informational interactions are clarified into a greater intent of Love.

You are a powerful biomechanism of choice. Your internal power is where all of your creation begins. Identify your intent, your internal alignment with what you want to create and experience in life. As that becomes aligned with your choices, look outward and observe the response from Life, for it is working with you for you to thrive.

Section Four

Light Language: Opening the Third Eye

Types of Light Language

This section will provide an overview of the different types of Light Language. It first details elemental Light Language, focusing mostly on elven and faerie, which are the most prevalent in terms of what people perceive. Next, angelic and galactic energies will be discussed in detail. This helps you recognize what you are drawn to and what you are accessing as you transmit or receive Light Language.

Chapter Eighteen

Overview of Light Language Categories

There are many varieties of Light Language. It is a communion with and through your Higher Self that allows you to access your timeless cosmic resonance. The Languages can be distinct and recognizable to a trained ear. You connect with energies that are significant for your life path and what needs to shift or expand. Each transmission is open to what is most appropriate for healing in the moment.

I have known people who have never met who channel the same Language, long before easy information about Light Language was available. These men and women have a similar resonance of life path and soul group that enables them to access the same Language and time stream.

There are Languages that have a strong resonance with physical healing, emotional healing or mental activation. Some Light Language has a resonance with certain time streams on Earth, such as Lemurian or Atlantean Languages. Some Languages are angelic, galactic, or elemental. Honor your specific path and what you are drawn to transmit and receive, as it will serve you, and perhaps others, with great momentum.

If you love working with animals, follow that love and allow Light Language to enhance your experience. You may be interested in a specific group of people, like children, veterans, Alzheimer's patients, or people who require physical or emotional healing. Notice what you are drawn to and notice what is drawn to you. It may continue to be part of your focus or just remain for a certain timeframe. As your Light Language and healing skills grow, your focus may change.

Light Language Origins

Throughout my interactions with Light Language over the years, I have noticed a general resonance of the energies that channel through me. At times there are energies of ancient Earth resonance. I have channeled galactic energies connected with specific indigenous cultures or different Earth-based cultures. I have tapped into streams of faerie energy that are resonant with Asian cultures (before I ever taught Light Language in Japan), and at other times the faerie energy did not have that specific connection. *Observe without worry about defining what you are experiencing. Notice with great fascination whatever you may sense.*

> *When you are speaking a language you know, you are utilizing your brain in a different way than you are with Light Language.*

There is a general umbrella of elemental, angelic, and galactic vibrations that transmit Light Language. Each of these can be composed of a wide variety of energies. This overview will demonstrate some of the differences, yet in truth, all the Languages are more similar than they are different. They all have the same purpose: to elevate humanity. They all heal. They all help people grow and have hope and excitement for the process and progress of Life. The separation is beneficial for understanding, and the connection continues as you reach higher into the oneness. You will naturally access the energies that are most beneficial for you. That may change over time, or even in a single transmission. There are times when I notice certain Languages dominating for a time period, and later find them becoming less prevalent.

Here are the various forms of Light Language:

> **Elven Light Language** focuses on heart/mind connection in order to bring the peace of high-level knowledge onto the earth plane. This opens science to its true nature of Love and Consciousness within all experience.

Faerie Light Language helps humanity open the heart and connect to Life through joyful reverence for All Life.

Angelic Light Language heals on a deeply emotional level; it reminds you that you are Divine, that you are sacred. This becomes the lens through which you view All Life.

Galactic Light Language activates an increase in excitement for expansion and progress—the passion of Life to evolve.

Ancient or Future Earth Light Language ignites memories, gifts, heals traumas, and works intimately with the human experience.

We will not go into detail about ancient or future Earth Languages (like Lemurian or Atlantean Languages), but it is possible to interact with Earth-based nonphysical energies as well. Most often, these Languages will not be recognizable as an exact earthly language, as Light Language is more layered than known Earth language. However, it is possible to access actual Earth languages you do not know (xenoglossia). *When you are speaking a language you know, you are utilizing your brain in a different way than you are with Light Language, whether the Light Language is glossolalia or xenoglossia.*

Though animals, crystals, elements, and all forms of life are able to communicate, they don't typically utilize the Language of Light (with the exception of whales and dolphins), though it is possible to connect with a species and access its original language. Because they reside here on Earth, they have developed communication with us. They typically communicate telepathically using imagery, emotion, and even our own words, especially domesticated animals. However, animals, crystals and nature generally love to receive Light Language, especially elemental and angelic Language of Light.

As you begin to practice Light Language, notice what is coming through. It can be such an exciting journey as you communicate with different energies. This connection is natural to us, though mostly forgotten through the glare of physical separation. Light Language helps expand you and others into cosmic human beings. You are not so separate from angels, elementals, and galactic races; you are resonant with them and merely exist in different form, different density.

All Life is part of God. As you find your inner angel, let that light love generously. As you find your inner elemental, let that light play joyously. As you find your inner galactic being, let that light illuminate brilliance here on Earth.

Chapter Nineteen

Elven Light Language

Many people feel a sense of reverie when they hear tales of faerie and elven realms. Why is that? Are they just fascinating stories, or is there more to it? Where did these stories originate? Skeptics may say they emerged from unintelligent people who couldn't comprehend how the sun and moon rose in the sky or how plants could bear fruit. That is simply not true.

Humanity has developed on Earth over much longer periods of time than mainstream history represents. Humanity has also had interaction with different cosmic races, but that is beyond the scope of this book. The elemental races have become fanciful legend, but their existence is rooted in a truth that has no proof. Trust your heart to guide you to what you feel is true.

As much as you could look at the different elements of nature as fulfilling certain human needs, the elemental races also do this for Earth and humanity. Their existence is not for this purpose alone, however; it is merely part of their make-up. In the past, they interacted with humanity closely. Before humans shut down their hearts and minds in this latest procession of time (yuga), they interacted peacefully and easily with the elemental races. Humans were able to see them because their eyes perceived a greater range of frequencies.

As the yugas descended, from fear of being outcast by those in power, people finally "agreed" to stop interacting with the elementals. Prior to this time, the elemental races (and some galactic races) helped humans understand and assimilate into agriculture, writing, cycles, weather indicators and much more. Each elemental race has a different proclivity of focus, with the elven and faerie races being the most pronounced.

Many people living today have DNA resonance with elven, faerie and other elemental races. You may have had many life experiences as part of these races, both on Earth and off, and you are now incarnated as a human. You can usually recognize your connection by a strong pull to pictures, stories or aspects of their focus. Often you can recognize those with strong elemental resonance by their physical appearance.

As an example, I was in a restaurant with some psychic friends and I spotted a human I sensed had prevalent ogre energy. I could see the overlay, but I didn't mention it. There was a sense of gentle giant in her being, even though she was sitting and didn't look overly tall. One of my psychic friends eventually turned around, saw her, and whispered, "Look, there's an ogre!" I appreciated the validation, as it was my first experience seeing a human with ogre resonance in real life. You could see the sweetness illuminating from this woman. What a treat.

I have met people of troll and leprechaun energy as well, though faerie and elven resonance are the most common. At times, it is difficult to differentiate between the two; many hold both energies, yet there are often discernable differences. As you read about the elven and faerie information in the following chapters, you will activate the resonance and understanding about them within you. Hearing and practicing their Languages of Light will further open you to your latent elemental gifts.

Elven Elementals

The elven are the bridgers. They bridge the angelic and the galactic energies, being somewhat of both, but closely related to galactic energies. They bridge nature and technology. The elven race is interwoven in the track of human history throughout many galaxies. They are a unique race that has had many incarnations of varying dimensional expressions and densities.

Their physical bodies do not vibrate at the same frequency spectrum as humans'. However, when they incarnate, they generally maintain physical bodies and their subtle bodies remain highly accessible to their physical structure. In other words, they are more aware of the subtle realm than humans are, and yet they are balanced in their focus on the physical. They integrate the subtle realms with ease while maintaining a strong physical focus. This manifests as a balance of meditative states that replenish and reinvigorate their physical and mental focus. Humans are able to access a similar state with activities like mediation, yoga, and connection with nature.

The elven races are master scientists of the dimensional expressions and they span technology from nature through evolution.

The elves are not as emotional as humans, though they do have feelings. Their emotional states are less intense than humans' because they have a strong, peaceful mental focus. For instance, they do not fear death like people do. They have less of an intense survival mechanism because their mental connection with the subtle realms is bridged by an emotional understanding of the eternal nature of Life. They do not forget or suppress memories like humans, so emotion doesn't overwhelm them. They maintain a balanced interaction with the logic of Life that is deeply aligned with emotional intelligence.

Life Sciences

The elven races are master scientists of the dimensional expressions and they span technology from nature through evolution. They understand the natural world with a depth of knowledge that humanity is just beginning to access with quantum theory. They understand the dimensional overlays, dimensional interactions, and how to tap into them to connect them to the physical. They have such a long history of life and a loving mental connection to it that they have the Akashic memory of the pros and cons of technological advancement.

The elven are also master geneticists. Their work with humanity has had many different expressions on various planets. Elven are adept at working with the elements of nature to change food (and even viruses) to upgrade the human structure. The elven race has absolutely no spirit of domination, however. They are so skilled with biological sciences and so connected with the timeless information of Life that they have no emotional lack creating a desire for domination. The elven are intricately connected with humanity through our cosmic heritage. This is their part in Polarity Integration.

Elven Interaction since Lyra

The elven race began humanity's interaction with the Akashic records, and they have been supporting our development through the eons since this expressional track of humanity began. The elven race began long before humanity's immersion through the *Prism of Lyra*.[1] As this track of humanity incarnated into form on Lyra eons ago, the elven assisted this evolution. In the first expression of humanity on Lyra, a minute amount of elven DNA was integrated into human DNA. It was a unique experiment of Polarity Integration that offered an understanding of how each race could evolve with varying degrees of its original traits. In many of the Lyran progeny, human DNA was much more dominant than elven. As the Lyrans evolved and spread to other planets, some experiences (like Sirius) had more dominant elven interaction.

As humans traversed many incarnations into physical form throughout the planets, varying degrees of elven genetics were implemented. Humanity and the elven race embarked upon this experiment together from the beginning, though the physical experiment was mainly for the human form. For example, the Orion experience had much of the intellectual intelligence with little of the emotional intelligence, so the use of technology to dominate others, even into other dimensions and timelines, got out of control. It eventually resulted in a human form with a strong biological pull to Love, and the Orion humans found their way back to balance.

For our Earth experience, which requires the integration of any imbalanced energy in our entire Akashic system, the elven (through the Sirian incarnational cycle) implemented the biological galactic time capsule into human DNA resonance. These biological

---

1 Lyssa Royal Holt and Keith Preist, *The Prism of Lyra*. Light Technology Publishing, Second Edition 2011.

galactic time capsules trigger the integration of your Akash, which is activated by certain parameters. These parameters mainly include reaching a certain vibrational resonance, but reaching a specific age or experience can also trigger a biological time capsule. In more recent years, the cosmic integration is also assisted by walk-ins, soul braids and incarnational/Higher Self overlays. We now have a wide variety of galactic DNA resonance available for integration and assistance.

Elven Wisdom

The elven race is like our wisdom. On this human track, we have chosen to experience a level of separation from the Life Source that has led to our divinity being forgotten. The elven agreed to participate with humans in order to hold space for remembering of that divinity to occur. Humans as spiritual beings have never forgotten their inherent divinity, but human form in current density allows for a forgetting that serves the reconnection. As humans evolved, the duality schism increased. Upon request, the elven integrated more of their mental capacity with humanity's through working with the natural sciences and positively affecting food, viruses, and interdimensional DNA structure. This helped to connect the human mind and heart; in other words, to connect human intelligence with an emotional moral compass.

Emotions connect. This is why the elven maintain such a balanced logic with the play of life. They honor emotions without being controlled by them or avoiding them, for they understand, through calm logic, the greater expanse of Life. Through elven interaction, humanity integrates science to improve life and connect the self with the broader spectrum of Life.

Elven Influence

Depending on your unique signature and the collective progress of humanity, each person is triggered in different ways in order to help evolve humanity. While some of this may come through past-life memory, most of it occurs in new and creative ways that apply to our current circumstances. Human scientists are influenced by their elemental resonance. Some inventions, philosophies, and creative endeavors are a result of these internal time capsules activating.

Anyone who feels a strong pull to J. R. R. Tolkien's book *The Hobbit* (and the series of books that followed) has quite a bit of elven resonance activated. These books were made into a series of movies because technology reached a point that it could more easily create a quality movie representation, and also because humans were ready for a more wide-scale activation of their elven DNA.

From my perspective, when Tolkien brought the books and the language of the elven through, he was a channel for activation of our elven (and other elemental) resonance. Tolkien's work, through unseen connections, inspires young scientists, inventors, philosophers, artists, farmers, and more. The elven connection stirs humans to evolve into greater cooperation with nature, balanced technological advancement, and a greater understanding of the unseen, timeless nature of Life.

Elven Light Language stimulates your resonance with technology and nature.

A beautiful aspect of Tolkien's contribution is the elven language that he brought into human consciousness. It is easy for a linguist (and for Tolkien himself) to logically track the influence of the language. Humans separate by country, tribe, skin color, gender, and in many other ways; but throughout history, humans were not so separate from each other. As humanity spread out across Earth, parts of different languages have been maintained, while other parts have been altered. As I perceive it, Tolkien merely distilled the elven language from the languages that were already in form. When you hear Tolkien's elven language, there is an immediate trigger of recognition, which in turn activates latent experiences that come to the surface in the most appropriate way.

Many say Tolkien's work was influenced by the war he participated in, yet the clearing and activating of the elven resonance was also meant to help humans clear the unconscious memories of pain from the massive Orion wars that reside in the Akashic records of humanity. The elven have also worked directly with humans since the fall of Atlantis to reinstate humanity's connection to our innate divinity. This was done on a personal level and with certain groups by connecting humans with the land and simpler technologies until people's moral compasses were more balanced with their intellectual capability.

When you hear elven Light Language, you are being spoken to in clear, direct terms because the elven are so interconnected to our DNA. The elven Language is much easier to interpret as it is more closely related to our own languages. It has taken a consistent track of connection throughout human incarnation.

Elven Light Language stimulates your resonance with technology and nature, with form and the formless. It stimulates a depth that is balanced in emotional flow and mental understanding. As you hear and speak elven Light Language, you open your mental capacities and balance them with healthier emotional flow. It is a powerful catalyst for remembering.

Chapter Twenty

Faerie Light Language

The first time I channeled faerie energy, I was shocked and almost embarrassed—though by that time I was generally over being embarrassed by the oddity of Light Language. I was teaching a class in Sedona, Arizona that ended up being all men. One of the men asked me if it was unusual to have all men in a class and I said, "Yes, and there must be a reason for it." There certainly was.

When I began channeling Light Language, a strong male energy came through that I would best describe as a galactic shaman. I could easily sense his cosmic signature and resonance to indigenous culture. I approached each male in the room as this galactic shaman lovingly but strongly berated and taught him in Light Language. This energy held nothing back, though no one but me consciously understood what he was saying. He went into great detail about how the Divine Masculine behaves in relationships, business, friendships, etc. It was a transmission to their hearts that they understood and received on an unconscious level.

> ***Faeries are the loving guardians of nature. They have a sweetness that is deeply based in love and joy.***

As that energy left, a new energy came in. I went from a deep, masculine voice and demeanor to a bouncy, high-pitched, percussive voice. I bounced around the room, dancing the words. It was embarrassing, but interesting. This energy felt like a faerie with a resonance with the earthly Asian cultures, though it also had a cosmic feel. First the galactic shaman, then the galactic faerie!

Whenever I channel faerie energy, they want to stay and play. They are the loving guardians of nature. They understand the cycles of life and they have a deep connection to the elven race. The best way to explain it is that the faerie are an offspring of the elven race that maintains a stronger emotional body.

FAERIE JOY

Faeries love to play! Their primary mission is to maintain the joy factor in life. They sing and play with the elements of the earth.

This is how faeries experience Earth:

Water is divine! Leaves are magnificent! Green leaves are fun! Changing leaves are exciting! The air is full of bubbles! Bird song is fanciful! It's a melodic complement to the babbling waters! Snowflakes are magic carpets! Raindrops are funhouse mirrors! The forest is sacred and light is in everything!

Light sings to the faeries and they derive much information from the color/octave of Light. It signals them to focus their joy with greater intensity or greater expanse. They will sometimes throw light at you (e.g., flash the dew on a leaf) to get your attention or even to nurture your energy field with a certain color frequency. Faeries are a vital part of the balance of life here on Earth.

Human Faeries

It is easy to recognize humans with a strong faerie resonance, though they appear similar to elven beings. Those of faerie connection want to be outside gardening, walking, playing and enjoying. They love animals and they love nature. Humans with faerie energy tend to see the best in people and are surprised when they are betrayed, though they forgive fairly easily, even if they keep a distance afterward.

Humans with faerie resonance like to sing and dance. They are fascinated by fire, water, smells and light. The fae have an obvious lightness; they focus on clean, clear things. Their dress tends to be light—simple and cute hairstyles, no heavy jewelry or makeup. Everything in their lives lends to a lightness of being. They tend to be vegetarian, humanitarian and at times frivolous. In human form, they may be a little uncomfortable unless they are able to shine with joy and play outside.

Perhaps you recognize some faerie energy within yourself.

Those of faerie energy or DNA do not typically incarnate into heavy family karma, though they can deal with human challenges on a lighter scale. Most humans will have a mix of energies, so even if you know you have faerie energy, you most likely have some other energies that will support your strength to deal with the earth plane in human form. People will activate their faerie energy at times when it is more plausible, either as a child or after they have left a challenging environment. Some only feel it when they are out in nature or playing with children and animals.

FAERIE WORK

Faeries have a sweetness that is deeply based in love and joy. Yet they have a rascally side as well. Sometimes this playfulness is misinterpreted by curmudgeons (they chose that word because it's a fun word!). Faeries are never mischievous with the goal of being harmful;

they are only roguish when someone is stuck and unable to find joy. This is an attempt to help that person stop harming him or herself with anger and unnecessary despair.

Faeries do not mourn like we do. When death occurs (which is merely a transformation of energy), they have two phases of what could be termed mourning: the Sacred Thank You and the Exaltation. The Sacred Thank You might seem mournful, and at times it is. It stirs a deep emotion of appreciation for Life in all its forms. It does not matter if the life or death was traumatic; it was beneficial. If the life or death was an easier experience, less emotion might come through in this song they sing, but not less Sacred Appreciation. Faeries have no regrets; they do not see as clearly into the Akashic records as the elven do, but they do not need to. They have an emotional innocence that is untainted by the forgetting of human form.

After the Sacred Thank You comes the Exaltation. This is a joyous celebration of Life and is the deepest form of respect for a life transformed through death. The Exaltation nurtures the information acquired by a life into the highest potentials that challenge or triumph can create. This creation is in the subtle realm and resides within the Akash, available for any human to access. When another human incarnates into physical form, he or she reads this information and makes soul path choices based on the needs of humanity derived from the Exaltation. Prior to incarnation, humans make unconscious soul choices to heal past challenges and expand past triumphs through the information of the Faerie Songs of Life.

Faerie Fun

Perhaps you recognize some faerie energy within yourself. If you would like to enhance and activate it, as well as learn to speak this type of Light Language, go outside. If you live in a city, find a park. If weather is not permitting, look out a window. If you only see high-rises and concrete, look at a picture or imagine a lovely scene. Find different natural environments to connect with the faerie realm, as they are anxious to play with you.

They know you, even if you do not know them. They read your energy like a book, as does all of nature. First, listen. Listen to the wind, listen to the water, listen to the leaves rustling *for you*. Soon you will sense the song of the flowers, the voice of the trees, and the nurturance of the dirt. Nature, thanks to the focus of the faeries, has never forgotten its joy. You may not see it, but it is there. In the depth of winter and the strength of a hurricane, it is there. Nature hears and sings a song you have to learn to hear. The dirt runs deep and no concrete can truly cover it. Being in nature is important for your health.

Faerie Light Language helps you remember your innocence and your exuberance for life. As you connect with their realm, you open your heart and bring a creative wonderment to yourself and other humans. Faeries are an emotional bridge. They help humanity hold a space of joy, excitement, play, creativity, appreciation, fascination, and responsibility with Life. As they like to put it, they are serious about joy! So get to it! Dance their Language and let it ripple and bounce through the bubbles in the air like rainbow joy!

Chapter Twenty One

Angelic Light Language

Angelic energy is interesting and an energy that is deeply entrenched in the human experience. Angels are a bridge to the Divine Source, something humans never lose, yet it can be easy to overlook. Although most people are a mix of angelic, elemental, and/or galactic, some are strongly angelic. The path of angel energy is healing and this is done mainly by giving assistance to others.

Angels support, connect, teach, and heal—that is how they connect you back to the Divine. Mother Teresa is an example of a person with strong angelic energy. She was in complete service to the Divine, and she was strongly driven to Love others into healing, one compassionate glance or touch at a time. That is what it is like to be an angel on Earth. Human angels are everywhere. Most often, the packaging isn't as evident as Mother Teresa's was, so look for them with your heart.

Angels don't fear to tread anywhere, but I meet many humans with strong angelic resonance who are timid with their energy field. Often this is because the angelic resonance results in an empathic quality that can quickly become overwhelming for a human. Many angelic humans work in hospitals and schools. They are generally less athletic and more emotional. They connect with deep compassion and give and give and give.

I remember meeting a human angel when I was giving psychic readings at a charity event in Los Angeles. This lovely lady sat at my table and as I connected with her energy field, I was met with such a loving vision that I began to cry. As best I could, I wanted to let her know my tears were because of the beautiful vision I was having, but I could hardly talk due to the massive influx of Love.

Finally, I regained my composure and told her, "You are an Angel sent here to Earth to Love the children. Your life is easier than most because you are meant to flow Love to the children." She agreed. Her husband was loving and made good money to support them. She worked at a school because she loved children, not because she had to work. She didn't have children of her own, so she worked in a school just to be around them. This is a fine example of how life experiences can be the perfect setup for us to live our unique dharma.

Angelic energy is focused on healing. Healing the separation within humanity is often done by being in a hospital setting, for example, and helping people heal physically, helping family members deal with loss, helping destructive systems change, or helping people die or be born. Often the angelic humans in these settings don't know the extent of the work they are doing, though this is changing rapidly as humanity's intuition increases. They are sometimes doctors, but mostly the angelics are nurses, counselors, and other hospital staff, because they want more connection with people. Those in the alternative medical fields (such as chiropractors, acupuncturists, and energy healers) are frequently angelic. Teachers are generally also of angelic resonance. Any type of service path draws a lot of human angels.

Protecting and Serving

It is imperative that those humans of angelic resonance build individual empowered boundaries because they are so empathic. They must keep their energy fields cleansed of others' issues and learn to use their energy wisely so they don't become depleted. That's easier said than done, although it is necessary for vitality. If you are strongly angelic, I recommend a few moments of intention in the morning before getting out of bed or leaving the house.

Visualize iridescent light surrounding you and repeat aloud:

> "My body and energy are protected through the Power of the Love of God (or Source, Divine Love, The Universe). This Light is my barrier of protection

that does not allow the depleting of my energy field by others. I do not process other people's energy with my body. I access the Infinite Wellspring of Grace and offer healing through Divine Sovereignty. My body is strong, protected, and available to assist in ways that support me and the greater Flow of Life. I am an instrument of Empowering Love."

Do this daily, even if you read it slowly. It's long because human angels have a big job! When you notice that you are not overly depleted throughout the day, it is set as a template in your energy field. You can then just visualize light around you and say something shorter, such as, "I am protected," "I am an instrument of Empowering Love," or any combination thereof. It will have the same meaning after the long version is templated into your energy field. Notice that this protection mantra isn't fear-based. It is a declaration of empowered Love that builds your strength to hold healthy boundaries that benefit all involved.

Angels are meant to heal and help people. Humans are meant to connect to each other and life. This is different from depleting yourself for others, which doesn't really help in the overall scheme of evolution as humanity evolves into empowered individuals creating empowered societies. There will be times when you give even though you feel tired, but these are exceptions, not a daily practice. With the aforementioned mantra, parents will still be connected to their children, and family or friends will still be connected with each other. The mantra creates a connection of empowerment that serves all, though each moment may not seem balanced.

It is a balance of being conscientious of what your energy field can handle (protecting it) and not feeling overly vulnerable, just as you understand that with a little wise precaution walking across a street can be safe. If you want additional support, visit https://jamyeprice.com/empath-support/.

Angelic Connection

Angelic Light Language is often the most beautiful and heart-touching. Those who sing the Language of Light usually sing angelic, elemental or ancient Earth languages (not always, just often). When Light Language is sung, it works deeply within the heart, often slowing a person down and assisting him or her in feeling an ancient memory or emotion, even if he or she is unaware of the details.

Angelic Light Language has a deep connection to divinity, as the main purpose of angels is to connect humanity with their Source within. Often, angelic Language of Light is not as easy to translate except in broad strokes, such as, "You are so Loved," "We Love you endlessly," and "Love yourself, you deserve it infinitely." Love, Love, Love and more Love. If you feel a strong resonance to angelic energy, plunge into empowered Love and you will find your energy, your voice, your health and your passion.

Light Language can help connect you to the angelic realms. Don't worry about what angel it is or what is being said; feel with your heart. The perfect energy will come to you and through you based on what you need. Get quiet and know that you are Divine, and allow the voice of the angels to Love through you.

Connecting with angelic Language of Light is a powerful experience, whether receiving it or transmitting it. Often when people first connect with angelic Light Language, they cry. That's perfect. The tears are releasing the pain of separation and opening your heart to the perfection of Life. Sometimes it is helpful to let it come through as a whisper first, so you are not shocked by your voice and still feel your heart connection. Sometimes it is helpful to play beautiful, gentle music, like harps or crystal bowls and let yourself sing along with it.

Every single person has access to angelic resonance. As you connect with this type of Light Language, you bring a powerful catalyst of Love onto the earth plane. You may not get to see the effect immediately, but you will come to understand that every word of Love uttered, even if heard by no one else but you, has a profound impact on Life. Let it flow through *you*.

Chapter Twenty Two

Galactic Light Language

Galactic Light Language can come from a large variety of species or even originate from different timelines among species. In general, it serves the purpose of physical and mental expansion to facilitate Ascension, as all Light Language does. You may often find that it seems intense. Typically, there is a little less obvious Love than with an angelic transmission, but that is only because of the focus of intellectual stimulation. Galactics usually focus on understanding the Universe, connecting, and teaching. They often are, or were, physical form-based beings, unlike many entities of the angelic realm.

Galactics don't play as much as the faeries. While joy is serious business to the faeries, education and progress is serious business to the interstellar races. They are the direct and indirect progenitors of the human race; our physical form is derived from them. Humans contain Akashic connections with many cosmic species: elven, faerie, other elementals, and angelic energies. This is unprovable, though eventually it will start to unfold—first from the galactic perspective.

STARSEED HISTORY

People with a strong cosmic resonance generally move rather fast, figuratively and sometimes literally. They don't like to stagnate. They like to discover, explore, integrate knowledge or experience, and then move on for more. They are fascinated by astronomy and science fiction, and they more easily recognize what is science fiction or what has a basis in distant memory.

The popularity of the *Star Trek* television show and movies is an example of a connection with a truth of our galactic citizenry. Not all the details of it are accurate, but I believe the core of what Gene Roddenberry brought through was based in a connection with the Akashic records. For example, humanity will move beyond fighting for resources, as well as the gender and race biases that separate or limit. There is a Federation of Planets/Species. Some of the more recent *Star Trek* series even access some written Light Language at times. The *Star Wars* saga is a reflection of the Orion experience of dark versus light, and a savior that healed the rift.

A wide variety of information is available about the different galactic races, with some species framed as absolute enemies of humans. Humanity is a culmination and mix of all the interstellar species that are interacting with this Polarity Integration experience. Anything purported to be in opposition to humanity should be dealt with in a way that integrates the experience into *empowered* Love. This is your experience of *internal* free will.

Light Language is a powerful catalyst for opening people to their cosmic heritage.

Pleaidians and Sirians are some of our most recent progenitors. However, the Lyrans are the first iteration of this human experience, and some find a resonance with the Vegan or Orion races as well. These are the main physical races humans identify with because of shared heritage.

Many people also resonate with the Arcturians, Andromedans, Antarians, Alpha Centaurians and more. In general, these are not part of the physical history of humanity, but the Akashic heritage. The Arcturians have been assisting our evolution since the Lyran incarnation, so there is a strong resonance with Arcturians for many people. The Andromedans are deeply connected to us as an overseer race that signals a stage of development that compels us forward.

Light Language is a powerful catalyst for opening people to their cosmic heritage. Most will not have conscious, direct memories, but there is often a familiarity and desire to learn more that comes with exposure to these Languages. Your galactic Light Language will come through you based on many factors. Your historical resonance is one main factor, and it influences the race(s) you bring through. For example, if you are working out karmic templates of the Orion conflict, you will transmit information that assists you with that healing. If you are working out a Lyran challenge, you will access the Lyran timeline that is appropriate to you. If you are activating a Sirian genetic time capsule, you will transmit encodements to assist that process.

Galactic Communication

Light Language is a catalyst for healing. It does this through heart understanding, shifting frequencies, healing emotional wounds, or putting you on a track of experience. This affects your DNA, for your DNA responds to the Language of Light directly. Galactic Light Language initiates fast movement through your biological technology in a loving reminder of the truth of your innate capability. Just as parents desire to feed and teach their children for their optimum experience, so do our benevolent interstellar brethren.

You have the choice within you as to how you will deal with Life. The path of Ascension requires you to command your internal free will and balance your external experience with a peaceful state. Choose your focus and choose it with power. As you hold a powerful intent to only allow supportive, helpful experiences that elevate humanity through the power of God's Love, you hold a healthy boundary of intent that is your Divine birthright. You can also choose to ignore it. Choose well. Love is the powerful compelling force within All Life, and eventually, All Life returns to Love. Our galactic forebearers remind us of this accelerated path.

As you intend to bring powerful, loving cosmic healing through, your altruistic heritage comes in to assist. As you intend to empower yourself and others, you have access to more advanced energies. As you seek admiration or grandeur, you bring in energies that provide that façade for you. Get clear and strong on what you want, because you attract it.

You are from the stars.

As you open to your galactic heritage by allowing Light Language to transmit through you, you assist your development and that of humanity in many ways. Galactic Light Language helps inspire new technology, cooperation, healing and progress in ways that can grow our human community beyond separation and into connection.

Perhaps as you open to galactic Light Language, you will go outside under the stars and allow loving information to flow through you. Do not fixate on what is being said or what race is coming through you at first. As you begin to recognize the feeling of this broad type of Light Language, you will eventually learn to discern its origin and information when applicable, either in detail or in general. The first step is intending with clarity, allowing without judgment, and then beginning the process of discerning information without worry. Practice and more practice follows.

Your intention to allow only benevolent and Loving energy through you opens your channel to the truth of Love from humanity's interstellar gene pool. You are from the stars. Bring that beautiful energy to Earth with great Love and care.

Section Five

Light Language: Releasing Fears

Channeling Light Language

This section begins with an *overview* (not an in-depth study, which is a valuable path) of conscious channeling, in both your known language and Light Language. It offers exercises to begin channeling safely and clearly. The following chapters detail how to practice channeling Light Language in verbal, signed, and written forms. It then offers information to help with translating Light Language, healing with it and representing it to others. It is a sacred responsibility to nurture its future for humanity. You are ready to begin a wonderful journey.

Chapter Twenty Three

Overview of Channeling

This chapter will provide an overview of conscious channeling in your known language and compare it to channeling Light Language. With conscious channeling, you stay aware of your body and surroundings. Humanity has progressed to a vibrational resonance that renders unconscious channeling unnecessary, though some people may still experience it.

For some, the basic instructions in this book will help you learn to channel Light Language. For others, more structured and extensive learning will be needed or desired. You can find information about learning to channel Light Language with me on my website, JamyePrice.com.

Before you engage in channeling, you must prepare yourself so you are clear about the energies you will allow to connect with you. This chapter helps provide a necessary foundation of what to observe as you are channeling, as well as some ways to begin to open your channel. The chapter entitled Angelic Light Language offered some valuable exercises for your healthy boundaries and wise, open heart. I recommend you reread that chapter and apply the exercises so your foundation of clarity is strong.

What Is Channeling?

We are all channels. The broad definition of channeling, just like the flow of water, is something vast tunneling into a more specific flow. Every being does this with the Higher Self, which is the vast, non-linear you, transducing into the physical, linear you. You are completely connected with your Higher Self and always receiving a flow of invisible energy (information) from your vastness into your specificness.

Understanding the broader definition of channeling is part of comprehending the broader nature of Light Language. Channeling is not just letting some far-away entity speak through you. Equivalently, Light Language is not just words that are verbalized or written. Channeling is a natural process of the vast, non-linear becoming manifest in the linear experience. What comes forward into the linear realm is the bridge between complete connection and definition for human understanding and expansion, or the wave becoming particle.

When a person is channeling, a connection beyond the linear, human self utilizes the mind to convey information. An artist painting an original picture experiences a similar process of channeling. If a painter is trying to duplicate a painting that has already been made, the mind usage is different. Rather than channeling, they are using mere technical skill.

You are allowing an information flow that is beyond your conscious mind.

When you are writing or speaking Light Language, you are in a state of expanded consciousness. This is not the same state as when you are speaking words in a conversation or writing words you know. Channeling the Language of Light is just like a true creative state, where you are not pre-planning nor are you accessing information you already know. *You are allowing an information flow that is beyond your conscious mind.* You are bridging your connected, non-linear self and your linear human self.

When a painter is in a creative state and channeling an original painting, the physical body is used to do the actual painting. Therefore, the person must either have enough confidence in his or her painting ability to let mind control go, or have enough of a desire to play with the paint without judgment. If the mind is in control, it will examine every brush stroke before, during and after. This limits even the painter who is confident in his or her technical painting ability. As you begin to channel, do not limit your flow by over-examining every detail.

Barriers to Channeling

The most common barrier to any type of channeling is the belief that it is not actually happening. Just as a painter picks up a paintbrush with great familiarity, that is how you channel. It is a familiar feeling; you allow your mouth to move and hear words come out of your mouth. But it is not exactly the same feeling as when you speak your own thoughts.

When you channel, you allow the words and movements to flow from a connection that does not originate in the conscious mind. This is similar to how the master painter moves the brush without examining every detail, but instead allows it to flow, knowing the ease and joy of discovery through a tuned instrument.

When you channel the spoken word in a language you know, the difference between the usage of the brain is definable to one who is comfortable with the process. Many people expect channeling to be wildly different from the self—such as an experience of complete omniscience. In some ways, this is the benefit of channeling Light Language. There is no preconceived notion about the words, so a person can be more open to allowing it to come through. For some it is easier than channeling in their known language; for others it is more difficult.

The human body system is created with the ability to discern deceptive energies—but only when the ego is not in control.

The biggest challenge for the beginner is to be open and allow without worrying if you can channel or not. The next biggest challenge is to be at peace with not knowing who is channeling through you or what is being said when you are channeling Light Language. *You open to channel more easily when you have no agenda, fear, or need*—just the strength of knowing your empowered Love. That takes practice.

CHANNELING WITH SAFETY

Some people who are new to channeling or unable to sense energies worry about what energies they will be connecting with—are they good or bad? I have a strong belief that All Life is God and God is unconditional Love. That does not mean every being, incarnate or not, is beneficial to interact with. I have done years of work clearing myself and setting intentions about what I am willing to experience. I do not strictly limit myself with the intent of who or what I will channel, I merely set parameters of what I do and do not want. For example, I want elevation for both humanity's highest good and my highest good.

Channeling Light Language is safe, as it is a pure transmission of Love. *Like all channeling, it also requires diligent personal work so your ego imbalances do not lead or influence your experience*, which is typically unconscious. I am in a constant state of observance of myself and I have outside help with my ongoing healing as well. Your personal healing and empowerment deserve some of your focus to build a strong foundation of security, courage, adaptability and humility with the process of channeling. I recommend continued effort and healing work to ensure your clarity.

The greatest impact of Light Language is the ability for the channel to trust into flow without filtering.

The human body system is created with the ability to discern deceptive energies—but only when the ego is not in control. You see this even in normal human-to-human communication. Some people can see through a manipulator, while others are oblivious to the manipulator's agenda. A controlling ego works two ways: it either convinces the person he or she is better than others, or it convinces the person he or she is not as good as others. Either way, an ego that is out of balance limits an individual's empowerment. A person with a balanced ego does not depend on being better than or less than someone else—he or she sees all people as unique. Personal empowerment is key to clear discernment.

You may notice some of your fears and insecurities coming up as you begin to channel. Observe yourself with detached compassion. Make new intentions and choices as necessary. Stretch yourself and nurture yourself. Practice alone to cultivate your strength. If you desire to share this practice with others, seek out supportive, open-minded friends to enhance your foundation of strength. Remember to use the powerful intent exercises that follow to help you strengthen and open your channel. You should use them continually for a while. You will need to use them less as your healthy boundaries become firmly established.

A Foundation of Trust

Light Language is a vast, intriguing topic. You are embarking on an exciting journey of personal discovery, universal connection, as well as fascinating information and experiences. As you maintain an open heart and wise mind, you help yourself to expand in a safe way that will also feel exciting.

The greatest impact of Light Language is the ability for the channel to trust into flow without filtering. Because the words that will be channeled have not been defined by an outside authority, there is no resistance to their meaning. Channeling Light Language does require an openness to the allowance of information that is not specifically understood by the conscious mind. It is an interaction with the powerful subconscious through the Higher Self. As a channel, your work is to allow without blocking the flow. As previously mentioned, this is in addition to a strong foundation of intent in which you only allow God's highest Love to channel through you.

As you become more skilled, you will be able to focus your mind on more details about what information is coming through you. However, to begin the channeling process, it is helpful to open your mind to your heart and trust your Higher Self for your benefit.

To increase your loving flow, look beyond the filter of, "I want to know who is talking," and into the filter of, "I recognize Love, and God's purest Love is all that is allowed to flow through me."

Look beyond the filter of, "I want to know what is being said," and into the filter of, "I understand with a depth that is beyond words, yet conscious understanding surfaces as appropriate."

Look beyond the filter of, "I want to know how and when my healing will manifest," and into the filter of, "Life is healing me in ways that are so magnificent that I am open to the perfect timing, the perfect path and the perfect synchronicities."

Look beyond the filter of, "People will think I'm weird," and into the filter of, "I have the wisdom of how and when to share something so sacred for the greatest benefit of all."

Setting Pure Intent

Having a pure intent for bringing through empowering, loving information is important to your channeling process. Pure intent relieves frustration, manipulation, stagnation and excitability. This is not to say there is no challenge in the process; rather, you are more focused on your empowerment and serving All Life (which includes the self) rather than serving the self through a veil of manipulation. One who has pure intent is calm, creative, detached, impassioned and has healthy boundaries that protect the self as well as keeping the self open to sharing.

How does one find this pure intent? *With diligent practice and patience as you continue to uncover any aspects of your ego that are keeping you in fear.* Having fear results in manipulation of the external world around you to establish security. Be patient with yourself; it can take time and effort to become aware of your pain and to change a pattern. You can focus your intent on becoming a clear channel of Love by stating the following:

> **"I am a pure channel of Love's expansion on Earth."**

With a deep connection to the words, repeat this slowly three times and see what you notice with your intuitive senses. Perhaps when you say "pure channel," you sense a feeling of lack of ability or a fear of judgment. Perhaps when you say "Love's expansion," you sense a feeling of the government holding you back or terrorists inhibiting freedom with fear. Perhaps you feel an excited stirring in your heart and throat, or a relaxation of the physical body.

As you observe these and continue to repeat the mantra, you will notice nuances that show you where you are out of balance with your empowerment, as well as what you are enhancing. Keep repeating this mantra each day until you feel no negative emotional charge with it, just a sense of empowerment: "I am a pure channel of Love's expansion on Earth."

Channeling is a natural process, and many people are balanced enough to discern if the energy they are bringing through feels Loving. If you do not sense or feel as you are channeling, you will notice by looking back with detached, loving observance. Did you feel like you were expanding yourself, tapping into something Divine and natural, even if you were wondering if you were doing it right? This is why it is good to practice alone or in nature at first—somewhere you feel comfortable. It strengthens your trust.

As you set your intent, "I am a pure channel for Love's expansion on Earth," you are beginning to open your conscious mind to your natural ability to connect beyond your thinking mind. Be patient with the channeling process if it is not natural to you. Don't try so hard to figure it out, just observe calmly and with the *joy of discovery*.

Chapter Twenty Four

Opening to Channeling Light Language

As you open to channel Light Language, you flood your physical body with Love that is beyond human words. Light Language is merely a unique form of channeling. All humans are natural channels; it is part of the natural functionality of your biomechanism—the physical and subtle body matrix. Your subtle body, your energy field, is communicating constantly. It receives, interprets, and emits information continuously at many levels.

Your subconscious mind is processing approximately 20 million units of informational data per second, while you are only conscious of about 40 units per second, according to Bruce Lipton in his

2005 book, *The Biology of Belief: Unleashing the Power of Consciousness, Matter, & Miracles.* That is just the purely Earth-based, normal informational processing of the brain. The subtle senses mimic the physical senses, thereby expanding them into greater connection. Channeling is one such subtle sense. It is a connection beyond the physical thinking mind, yet it is a connection through your Higher Self. Within your DNA resides the capability to receive, interpret and emit information. Channeling brings vast information into conscious expression.

Because of the Higher Self filter, it is impossible to unconsciously surrender your free will to Light Language or any energy coming through Light Language. It occurs because within the instructions of your DNA is the capability to receive non-linear information flow. This is the basis of the Law of Resonance, that you experience as your comprehensive vibrational resonance allows. Any experience will have a beneficial teaching of resonance and clarity evolving. Many people find that Light Language will start spontaneously coming through them, even though, prior to that moment, they did not consciously choose it. This is because there was a soul agreement to experience it. From that point forward, at any time, you have conscious free will to stop allowing it through you. Just as I told the story of the girl who went to a shaman to remove the ability to channel Light Language, you can do so with your pure intent (or find a shaman to assist you). Source will honor your decision and will not punish you. If you change your mind at a later date, that will be honored, too.

Humanity is experiencing an interesting time of evolution as we are immersed in the magnetics of an escalating energetic yuga. We are actualizing a development of stronger conscious connection with the subtle realm. Intuitive senses are increasing. A desire for loving connection and empowerment is growing. This is a natural evolution that is at an interesting collective resonance of expanded conscious non-linear communication. Light Language expanding heralds this change.

Beginning Observation

As you prepare to channel Light Language, observe and ask yourself questions. Do you notice thoughts or feelings surfacing? Do you begin to see or hear the Language of Light in your mind? Do you sense physical feelings in your body, like your heart area tingling or heat emanating from your hands? Does your throat tingle? Do you have the desire to move your head in gentle circles or move your hands slowly? You may want to practice channeling by writing Light Language, which can start with a doodle and then morph. Did you know many artists work this way? Be open to how you channel naturally.

Set the intention for Love to flow through you in the form of Light Language and observe what transpires.

Remember, channeling Light Language is merely a unique form of channeling. Instead of writing words or symbols that are familiar, you are opening to the informational flow of the universe. Instead of speaking words you know, you are allowing the informational flow of the universe to speak through you. This is filtered through your Higher Self, and conveys vast information in a way that is greater than the conscious mind can easily define.

As you channel the Language of Light, it is helpful to keep a sense of wonderment about the process, which keeps you open to flow and excited about discovery. The opposite of that is a shutdown of your flow as the mental body tries too hard to define what is being said or who is saying it. Allow your discovery to unfold in the proper time.

Some forms of Light Language (written, spoken, sung, or signed) may be easier for you at first, while others may seem more difficult. You may have aspects you never open to in this life. I know successful channelers of Light Language who do not channel every form. They are typically skilled in a particular area and feel no sense of lack about it. There are people who can translate it without being able to channel it. It is possible to open to Light Language in many different ways, so allow your journey to unfold with ease.

One person can channel many different Languages, though some will channel only one. What I find happens most often is that a dominant Language (or two) will channel through first because you are most resonant with it. It may change over time. You may notice you are channeling a specific

Language for a while, and then you move past it. Not because one is lesser than the other; they are just different Languages.

When you channel Light Language for other people, you may speak in Languages that are common to their soul streams. You may notice you access different energies and Languages based on what you are working on healing or understanding. You may access an ancient Earth Language because you are working with a time stream and cultural experience that matches the resonance of that Language.

Sometimes the Languages will change during a single transmission. For instance, it may shift from a Pleiadian to an Andromedan transmission. During that transmission the Language may change, or it may stay the same even though the energy channeling through has changed. This means the energies are communicating in a Light Language you are familiar with, rather than their own. I often experience groups of energies transmitting at once. Enjoy watching the experience unfold!

Practicing Channeling Light Language

A wonderful way to practice and support the flow of Light Language frequencies is in nature. Nature is always receptive. When you go out in nature, the plants and trees interact with your energy field, initiating healing and opening of your field. The ions in the air affect your physical body, nurturing your cells in magnificent ways.

Set the intention for Love to flow through you in the form of Light Language and observe what transpires. Do you feel the desire to sing, move your hands, or speak? Just let it flow. You are in the realm of the elementals; they will help you. Play with them. Enjoy your discovery and openness as you flow the Language of Light with joy and without any sort of agenda or fear. The flowers are laughing with you, not at you! All of nature is very much alive and able to communicate with you in different ways: the play of light, the arrival of an animal, a message in your known language, or Light Language that flows spontaneously.

You may find it natural to practice with animals. Some animals are open to it; others aren't. It can be too intense for them sometimes, so I recommend trying it and seeing if they want it. They generally prefer angelic or elemental Light Language, often in ways that don't have jarring movements or sounds.

It is important to practice alone at times so you build your inner knowing and empowered connection. If you do not desire to share Light Language with others, that is perfectly fine. You will still have a magnificent journey and improve the human experience. If you do desire to share with others, your next step is finding willing, open-minded, and supportive friends and family to share it with.

As you share it with others, you may experience synchronicities that help you know you are accessing Light Language. You may get an impression of something the Light Language is doing—perhaps working on the knee—and then the person will validate they either had a knee issue, or they felt that, too.

Opening to Channeling Light Language | 249

Sometimes you will not receive validation. That is fine. Trust and keep practicing. Sometimes validation is the best support, and sometimes no validation is the best support. I spent almost two years not even knowing that I was channeling Light Language, even though I could easily speak with my Guides. I trusted, I allowed and I kept my heart open to the answers when they came. Your journey may be faster and easier in many ways, but it will be your unique journey. Keep your heart and mind open to its unfolding.

As you allow Light Language to flow through you, you may notice that certain places or events may cause it to flow automatically. If you are learning Light Language for your own personal usage, this does not need to be part of your experience. For example, if you go to a spiritual workshop, sacred site, or hospital, you may notice the frequencies running through you. You will be able to control how it runs through you for the most part. As a representative of Light Language, your careful consideration of others and the honoring of the energy flow are important. It is important to balance the energy of not hiding yourself, not acting out for attention, as well as honoring others and the environment you are in.

Remain open to your unique path with channeling Light Language. Do not compare yourself to the experience of another in ways that make you feel less-than. There is a beautiful reason for each person's unique path. Be well with your path; it will begin with challenges and strengths. If you find a strength or a glimmer of a strength, enhance it and let the other ways unfold in the background. If you find a challenge—such as speaking it is difficult, but writing it is easy—keep testing your speaking abilities occasionally while you focus mainly on developing your writing.

You are capable because you are Divinity. You are learning because you are a human being.

Ask to experience the challenging aspects in your dream state, to release any fear about being right or being perfect. Observe your feelings, be authentic, nurture yourself, and stretch yourself through improvements. You are capable because you are Divinity. You are learning because you are a human being. These two are completely compatible and perfect.

Enjoy your unique journey of opening to Light Language. Relax into it. Trust and honor your path. It is going to be sweetly exciting and perfectly challenging. All of it supports you and calls you to your empowerment. It has a much broader scope of expansion for your life than just the ability to transmit Light Language. It is one part of the beautiful and sometimes challenging journey of Ascension. It is an expansion into more of what you already are: a Divine human being.

Chapter Twenty Five

Finding Your Voice

Every person on Earth is a natural channel of energy. We are constantly emitting, interpreting and receiving vibrational signals. Humanity's biological make-up is created specifically to facilitate this. The subtle world your intuitive senses receive has a different balance of density than the physical world; therefore, as you delve into the subtle realm, you are working in a more malleable density of form. This is the nature of Light Language; it is less dense in form than the languages we speak on Earth.

In our earthly languages, an agreed-upon association with words gives density to their meaning. The energy transmitted with your regular language is adapted by a person's association with it. As it reaches the person's energy field, the frequencies interact and cause a vibrational reaction based on his or her association, often unconsciously. For instance, when a person who has been abused receives the word "love," he or she may have a strong aversion to the word and block its benefit.

> *Light Language is a transmission of energy, not just a flow of words coming out of your mouth.*

Part of the beauty of Light Language is that you can transmit a purity of information because your association with the words is not as dense. For this reason it is imperative not to focus on the translation of the words as you open to channeling Light Language. If translation comes, so be it. If it does not, it will most likely come eventually. Your *patience and practice* with channeling the Language of Light increases your ability to interpret the information and energy you are receiving. Once you are more secure in your capacity to channel Light Language, you can begin to focus more on understanding the meaning of the transmission.

Recognizing Light Language

The difference between Light Language and just uttering nonsensical sounds is the energy flow. *Light Language is a transmission of energy*, not just a flow of words coming out of your mouth. The Language of Light contains vast quantities of information, some of which can be interpreted into words for logical understanding, some of which cannot.

You are opening to a flow of energy, not *just* saying words from another language. Therefore, you will *feel* Light Language as a different frequency than when you are just speaking words. The stronger your physical vessel is for channeling energy, the more information you can transmit with your Light Language. In the beginning, your Light Language will not have as much clarity, just as one learning a language becomes better over time. Your ability to channel will strengthen and expand with practice. Your personal healing is a vital component of your clarity and growth.

As you first begin to channel Light Language, the biggest hurdle for most people is allowing it to come through and believing you are truly channeling rather than just saying random words. As you practice alone, you build trust, clarity, and your interpretation faculties. You are clearing and strengthening your channel.

Your first step in interpreting is usually a physical or emotional sensation that something different is happening. These physical sensations may feel like a tingling, a warmth, or a buzzing. The emotional sensations may feel like a stirring in the heart, a memory of familiarity that can't quite be placed, a yearning or an embrace. Become astute to these signals, as they may be subtle.

Beginning with Light Language

When channeling, it is helpful to be in a place where you feel absolutely free to make noise or move around. This may be in nature or a room in your house. You may want to close your eyes as you first transmit Light Language verbally, as it puts you in a slightly different brainwave state and focus. You may want to whisper so you don't shift your brainwave state too much as sound first begins to flow.

Sit for a moment and set your intention aloud:

"I am open to speaking or singing Light Language. The Light Language that comes through me is the purity of Love manifest."

Sit quietly and see what you notice. You may feel stirrings in your physical body around the throat or heart. You may hear something in your mind.

A few tricks that are helpful for beginners are to put a hand (or both) on the heart, or to open your hands with your palms facing the sky. These are signals to your subconscious mind that you are opening your heart or opening to receive.

You may hear words in your head, or you may not. If you do, repeat them without worrying if you are getting them right. As you begin to repeat them or a portion of them, you allow your voice, throat, and physical vehicle to begin transmitting Light Language aloud. Without thinking too much about it, continue speaking or singing, however it is coming out of you. As you continue practicing, you are clearing and strengthening your channel.

Do not concern yourself with "who" you are channeling or what you are saying; your Higher Self is protecting you and will only allow Love manifest to transmit through you, as you intended clearly. Keep allowing the flow to happen without judgment about how weird it may seem. If you feel more comfortable whispering, honor that, for your heart often speaks in whisper. You may find it helpful to rock your body slowly and gently; this can help move you into a deeper trance state, though you are still aware in this state.

If you do not sense any words coming, you can repeat *slowly*, "Eeshah, ehmah, ehtah." This is a Lyran/Pleiadian prayer that equivocates to, "I receive you (All), I Love you eternally (All), I continue your Love forward." It is a connection to the foundational function of Life, your part in it, and your connection to All Life. It is a profound opener of the heart on levels that help to clear the channel of resistance to the power of Love.

As you repeat this prayer slowly, you may naturally start allowing more words through. You can put your hand on your heart or open your palms and observe how your physical body and emotions feel as you poignantly say these words. If you merely do this exercise for a few moments each morning, your vibration will begin to change steadily.

You may find that singing Light Language is easier for you than speaking it. This can vary by person or even in the moment. However it naturally occurs for you is fine. Singing is a powerful emotional experience and for some it helps open the flow as more senses become involved. Sometimes it is helpful to make a sound, like a tone, and then begin speaking or singing Light Language. Playing soothing music like harps or crystal bowls may help open your flow as well.

Practice Is Imperative

The most important part of learning to channel is practice. What feels unknown at first becomes clear as you grow more confident discerning when you are channeling. Your work is to practice and allow yourself to grow without stilting your development by overanalyzing or judging yourself too much.

Allow, observe, and enjoy the process. If you hear it in your mind first and then repeat it, be open to that changing over time. If you are more comfortable whispering it, practice speaking it aloud occasionally so you strengthen your channel to be able to adjust to the needs of the moment.

After you have become comfortable practicing by yourself, you may want to share with an open-minded friend. It is helpful to feel safe and supported as you are doing this. If you find your friend is not supportive, stop practicing Light Language with them, but don't give up. If you feel scared to share it, that is perfectly normal.

If this is just for you, that's perfectly fine, too. Even if you are just hearing it in your head and never share it aloud, it can be helpful on your life path. Just observe what feels right for you. My own path was best served by sharing it aloud. For an attorney, letting it silently flow within as appropriate is a more powerful path than forcing the integration of Light Language into closing arguments. That attorney will be able to assist people with the Language of Light (silently, through Higher Self agreement) in a way I would likely never be able to reach. Honor your path.

Continue to practice allowing words and songs to channel through you with your intent of transmitting Light Language. Practice with your eyes open and closed. Notice any sensations you feel as you transmit it. Start to notice if you sense galactic energies, elemental energies, or angelic energies. Don't worry if you don't have a sense of that; remember, your Higher Self is filtering energies for your best good, and your interpretation skills will improve over time.

You are transmitting only Love manifest when you allow Light Language to come into your life. Enjoy the practicing phase with the knowing that it will progress. With a great poignancy, appreciate the opening aspect of your channel, for you are helping humanity to expand just by your own willingness—even if you never utter Light Language to another. You are in a time of great transformation, and therefore, service.

Chapter Twenty Six

Moving the Energy

When I first began channeling Light Language, it came through my hands. I was working on clients who were lying on a massage table with their eyes closed. I began to notice twitches in my body and hands. Though I didn't know it at the time, I am a full-body channel. Just as a voice channel receives signals they interpret into words, my entire body receives energy signals that it interprets into movement as a response to the energies that are working through me. Most often you will be physically transmitting Light Language through your hands and mouth.

When Light Language transmits through your hands into the field around you, sometimes you are writing Light Language into the energy field and sometimes you are transmitting energy through specific pathway formations. For instance, my hands will automatically go into certain known mudras, like touching the thumb to the middle finger. This specific energy pathway formation has various meanings to it, but the movement is appropriate for the information. Much like a triangle has a multitude of meaning within it, so does the Light Language that signs through your hands. At other times, I write Light Language, an actual written Language, in the air. I have seen those who write the same Languages on paper that I write in the air.

As you practiced speaking and singing the words, I recommended that you put your hand on your heart or turn your palms up. Now take that a step further. Without worrying about which hand is supposed to do what, put one hand palm up and one hand palm forward. Do not stop to think about it, just do it. One up, one out. If you have previously learned that one hand gives energy and one hand receives energy, note that this does not apply to signing Light Language. The Languages transmit based on the energy flow that is necessary for the intent.

You may have a dominant hand that signs (writes) Light Language in the air. You will eventually be able to use both with practice. The reason I am guiding you to put one hand palm up and one palm out is to offer energetic support for the flow of energy. Your palm-up hand helps you balance the reception of energy and your palm-out hand transmits outward. This is different than the idea that one hand gives and one hand receives; here, one hand stabilizes and one hand transmits. Your stabilizing hand does not need to remain still. This is merely a beginning exercise.

Now that you have one hand palm up and one hand palm out, allow your hands to be gently moved by the energy flowing through them. Notice any sensations you feel in your hands. Do you feel a tugging of energy? Do you see your hands moving in your mind's eye, even though they are not moving? You may notice that your hands move on their own, or you may not have that experience at first.

Let it Flow Slowly

Begin to move your hands slowly and gently. Do not worry about doing it correctly or what you are signing and writing in the air. Even though in this instance you are initiating the movement yourself, you are actually opening to the movement of the energy flow. Just as speaking the words can start the flow of the words while channeling, sometimes you must gently move your hands to begin the flow of the energy. All of these exercises are about allowing, though at times the opening of your channel comes through your active direction to allow.

Keep moving your hand (or hands) gently and slowly until you feel an impulse that feels ever so slightly as if your hand is "wanting" to move in a certain way. Most often these will be small movements at first and will not look anything like letters, words, or the way my hands move in my videos.[1]

If you are right-handed in your normal life, there is no formula defining that Light Language will naturally sign with the same or opposite hand. What you

---

1 Visit JamyePrice.com/videos

are doing in this process of signing Light Language is allowing the flow of the energy to move your hands, not the direction of your brain. That is completely different from writing words you know.

You are learning to let the energy control the movement of your hands.

You are learning to let the energy control the movement of your hands. At first the movements will likely be smaller and slower until your hands are freer to move without your focus. Just as your handwriting was slower, larger, and less refined when you were a child, you will refine the movements of your hands naturally as your channel opens further. Slower movement helps you sense subtle energy. Observe as your hands give you gentle signals as to the flow of energy. You may notice movement repeating as your channel is opening, clearing, and strengthening. When you let the process interest you, you maintain an open energy field. Don't worry about being perfect or profound.

If signing Light Language is meant to be part of your path, you will continue to improve your skills. If you practice and still do not feel the energy moving your hands for you, please let it go with Love and peace, and know there is a beauty and perfection to every individual path. Some people only sign Light Language, while others never do. Perhaps later you can try again, when you feel more confident because you are well versed in another format. Often the hand movements can open after writing Light Language on paper. As you release any frustration about your abilities, you open yourself to your unique gifts. Trust your path. It is Divine.

Chapter Twenty Seven

Writing the Energy

There are many different forms of Light Language that can be spoken, sung, signed and written. Your written Light Language may look different from anything you have come across before. When you channel the Language of Light, you access streams of time or Languages of energies that vary. For example, Pleiadian Language will not always look or sound the same because it evolves over time, just as our Earth languages change.

Energy and information are within all symbols, though not all symbols are technically Light Language as we open to this layer of non-linear information flow. The Language of Light is a transmission of actual channeled Language and energy which has a volume of information upon it that is beyond the scope of mere words. As you begin to channel written Light Language, it is helpful to become clear about your openness to allow.

It is beneficial to observe written Light Language by others, but it is also important to remain open to yours being different from what you have seen. I have seen Light Language that looks like nothing more than a squiggle, and yet it is powerful Light Language. I have seen squiggles that absolutely are not the Language of Light. I have seen Light Language that looks somewhat picturesque, and pictures that are not Light Language. You discern the difference through the transmission of the energy and information.

While learning to channel written Light Language, it is important to allow it to flow onto the paper without judgment. Your channel opens when you put pen to paper and allow yourself to write or draw as you sense what you are feeling. The mere act of intending and doing begins to release blocks to your channel and improves your ability to access Light Language over time.

When children are learning to write, their writing is normally large and shaky. They are establishing mental clarity and fine motor skills. You have an advantage because you already have fine motor skills, but remember that you are still learning a new skill that will become more refined over time. Some people are natural channels and writing flows easily from them. Most must learn to balance opening and allowing. It takes time to hone this skill, so keep practicing.

When I teach Light Language in person, I notice that many beginners will repeat patterns and flowing shapes rather than write actual Light Language.

This is just a normal process of the channel opening. There is healing happening, and often either I can tell them what was healing from their transmission, or the person channeling it tells me. Often, after some practice with this, they begin to form Light Language. First it may be just a small part of the whole written transmission, but I am frequently amazed at how quickly people progress in class.

Though my natural opening to Light Language was through the hands, it was a much different experience signing it in the air than writing it on paper while holding a pen. My hands were used to a three-dimensional space and a much larger scale than a piece of paper. With practice, my skills expanded and refined to incorporate more. Practice will serve you well, too.

Writing Light Language

There are many different ways to practice writing Light Language in the following paragraphs. Try some different methods and find what feels most expansive to you. Allow it to change over time as well. As you notice the nuances of what keeps you open to flow and enjoying the process, you find your natural way of channeling.

One way to practice writing Light Language is to begin doodling on a page. As you move the pen with no agenda except the intention to channel Light Language, you are beginning to open your channel. Some Light Language looks more symbolic, while other forms look more like unrecognizable letters. Sometimes it looks similar to some of our older Earth languages like Sanskrit, Chinese, or Hebrew.

You do not need to use your non-dominant hand, but if you feel inspired to try that, follow your heart. You may find it easier to look away from the page, blur your eyes on the page a bit, or neither of those may work for you. You may see Light Language in your mind's eye and then replicate it as closely as possible.

Writing Light Language is a quiet and personal experience.

My personal experience with writing it was that I first saw nothing in my mind's eye and had to just let my hand move. After practice with that, I got a sense as to what was being transmitted. It looked like symbols, lines or shapes. Then over time I began to write as if I were writing a letter to someone, just continuous writing. Sometimes I had no idea of what was being transmitted, sometimes I did. Eventually, I could also bring through detailed symbols that I would see in three dimensions and in motion in my mind, and I would draw them. It still continues to evolve, at least in my experience, so be open to your path changing and growing.

Sense what you are feeling when you look at your written transmission. You may be feeling such strong judgment about its validity or perfection that it is hard to feel what you are reading on the paper. You may want to observe written Light Language and emulate it without trying to copy it exactly. You may want to practice in nature so you receive the benefit of nature assisting the opening of your energy field.

Written language is a denser form of communication than spoken language. As you practice writing Light Language, you anchor higher-dimensional frequencies in a format that has a strong structure and is beneficial for continual work in the energy field. Set some intentions about what you want to transmit and keep them around your house. Perhaps you could write a transmission about your home being a peaceful environment that supports loving relationships. Watch the energy change as your Light Language works to shift the vibration around you.

Writing Light Language is a quiet and personal experience. For some, sound or movement may be jarring and break the meditative channel connection. Each form has its value, though I find writing to be easiest for many people because they have a more internal expression on paper. It also gives you tangible focus and provides a written catalogue of your improvement. Your experience with writing can unfold volumes of information for you and clearly show you that you are capable of channeling Light Language. Enjoy the practice and growth.

Chapter Twenty Eight

Translating Light Language

Translating Light Language is exciting, but as you begin to learn how to channel it, it is important not to let a desire to "know" stifle your ability to channel if it is not natural to you. People who have too strong of a mental body controlling their creativity will have a harder time channeling. Sometimes they will be able to access Light Language, and then the mental body will shut down the channel because of too much emphasis on who or what is being channeled too soon. I have seen it happen to people. The good news is you can work yourself back into a state of allowance.

As you rework your filters of allowance to be congruent with the flow of Love, interpretation will activate as applicable. I have met people who are able to translate Light Language without being able to transmit it. Your path will be appropriate for you, best for you and it will also change. Over the years I learned to translate Light Language well, but even with that capability, I do not always know all of the information. There are still transmissions where I get no impressions of information, only appropriateness. Be at peace with how it opens in you.

Remember, Light Language often isn't a word-for-word transmission, so usually you will not get a stream of linear words as the translation, though that does happen occasionally (most frequently with elemental Languages).

If you are over-thinking it, you will close off your channel.

You begin to translate Light Language by observing the sensory data you are receiving. Sensory data comes in all different ways and it is a matter of recognizing how your intuitive senses speak to you. Intuitive senses are generally subtle rather than obvious, and they build with usage. Be aware of the ego, which is well-versed at negating experiences and blocking your flow with judgment and doubt.

Most often I find that people don't recognize much of their psychic data due to expectations about its intensity and profundity. For instance, a clairvoyant vision does not overtake your entire experience. It is in your mind (though sometimes visible outside of the mind) and similar to a thought, but slightly different. Often it is accompanied by an unusual and subtle feeling or insight that you must learn to recognize.

Your psychic senses are as unique as you are. Just as some people have a natural ability to run fast or sing beautifully, you will have natural psychic abilities that are specific to you. You can also work with them and make them stronger and more accessible for you, just as one practices to be able to run faster or sing better. It takes practicing with your intuitive senses to begin to notice your own subtleties, as well as to trust them.

Sometimes the trust builds as you practice with others and receive outside validation. After a while, you become astute at recognizing and trusting your intuition. Sometimes trusting your psychic senses means learning when not to take them literally, but to look for different metaphors until you get it right. Your psychic senses do not communicate in absolutes at all times.

Observing Sensory Data

When you are transmitting or receiving Light Language, there is a vast information flow. Rather than just seeking words in a linear form or the name of the energy speaking (which may not even be applicable), look first for the foundation of the information flowing. Whenever you interact with channeled material, notice the subtle nuances of the information flow beyond the words being spoken. This subtle energetic of greater connection is key to channeling. This also begins to strengthen your discernment of what is beneficial for you and what is not.

To begin looking for the information of a Light Language transmission, observe what you are noticing in your physical, mental, and emotional bodies. Are you suddenly hot, cold, or feeling tingling sensations? Do you notice odd thoughts surfacing, like a memory of a situation you haven't thought about in years? Are you feeling a sensation of peace, sorrow or a feeling of "home?"

If you have a sense of what is being transmitted, trust it and be patient with it. If you feel a sense of peace, trust that the transmission is easing your flow with Life. Perhaps after a transmission, you found yourself thinking about your mother, even if it is a little while later. That transmission was clearing some issues between you and your mother that blocked your ability to find your peace.

In addition to looking for sensory data from your intuitive senses, you may want to gently begin to discern if you are sensing angelic, galactic, elemental or Earth-based energies. Sometimes it is helpful to share with supportive intuitive friends who can validate what they are feeling and sensing. You may notice a few words in your own language, or a general sense of what is being transmitted. You may have a sense of who is transmitting. You may see symbols or images telling a story. When the information flow is an exciting validation rather than a necessity, it is helpful. You will begin to notice that Light Language is speaking to you in many varied intuitive ways.

PAY ATTENTION WITH EASE

Allow the translation of Light Language to unfold gently for you. If you are over-thinking it, you will close off your channel. I noticed this when I began to channel in English. I can hear what is being said as I channel. Sometimes it would interest me so much that I would start thinking about it. I quickly noticed how my own thinking limited the channeling, because I was pulling the usage of my brain away from the channel, which is a very different flow than channeling the Language of Light. When I channel Light Language, I am accustomed to paying attention to a large amount of data flow while the Light Language is coming out of my mouth and moving my hands and body. When I channel in English, it is different for me and I cannot pay attention in the same way.

As you get more comfortable channeling Light Language, focus on remaining peaceful and excited about how the process will unfold and improve. This will enhance your openness to the flow of information. I find that everyone I've encountered who channels Light Language is eventually able to receive some sort of a translation. You will open to it as well. Enjoy the discovery process as it unfolds for you. Seek answers with the balance of remaining open before an answer comes.

When you interact with Light Language, you are in constant contact with your expansion through the unknown, the new. You will be called to be empowered, step by step, and to help empower others. You will be teaching by example of what it means to open to the unknown, to discover the unknown and to repeat that process with joy and reverence in many areas of your life. Light Language is helping you understand the language of the future unfolding. It is a peaceful unknowing with the knowledge that all is well. Paradox again. What a blessing.

Chapter Twenty Nine

Healing with Light Language

As you interact with Light Language, you begin a healing process that is largely invisible. All change happens invisibly at first; creation begins in the subtle, unseen realms. Healing with Light Language is an exciting aspect of what humanity is moving into—creative interplay and trust with the unknown, for it is known in the timeless, connective heart.

The Language of Light points to the value in what is beneath the obvious—a connection with Life on unexplainable levels. It brings a remembrance of our true history and an opening to capabilities we are just beginning to rediscover. Light Language is one aspect of Life's beautiful mystery—and so much more.

Finding Your Path

It is important to practice in ways that make you feel confident about your ability to transmit Light Language well. Practicing by yourself on your own personal healing is important to strengthen your connection and confidence. When you feel you want to begin practicing with others, find supportive friends who are open-minded and intuitive. Also practice on some who aren't as intuitive, but just as open-minded. Have fun with the process. You will develop natural ways of working that feel right to you.

Whatever you choose, I recommend you work on people in person as you are beginning. Once you have strengthened your abilities and intuition enough, you may desire to work via distance. Part of the value of working directly with people is the debriefing experience as you both share what you experienced during the transmission. Other's experiences and reactions will help you validate that you are transmitting Light Language as your confidence grows.

Sometimes other people's lack of intuitive information will be the perfect challenge that shows you how much you trust yourself without reliance from the outside. The telephone or a video platform is beneficial for distance work. It is helpful to learn how quantum we are, but that comes with grounded knowledge in the physical experience.

How to Heal with Light Language

Because the Language of Light can be written, spoken, sung, or signed, there are many different ways you can choose to facilitate healing with it. Utilize your natural strength(s) and you may or may not want to stretch into forms of Light Language that aren't as easy for you. Personal healing is vitally important, especially if you are or would like to work on others. It is imperative to continue your own improvement so that you aren't avoiding your healing by focusing on others.

During a healing session you may want to write a transmission. Maybe you prefer to sing, speak, or sign it. You can begin with allowing spoken transmissions to flow through without any intention as to what is healing, or you can focus on a topic you would like to heal. You may combine written and spoken transmissions. You may find that angelic energy comes through you often, or that you always have a sense of galactic history. Practice in many different ways and enjoy observing what you discover.

Appreciate the process however it shows up. It is working *for* you at all times. You will likely find others who are transmitting Light Language as I did in the beginning of my journey. Working with them will be beneficial to your expansion as you support each other into faster growth. There is great value in working alone and with others—it is the balance of separation and connection.

TRUSTING YOUR PATH

Receiving and transmitting Light Language is a wonderful experience. Usually when you are opening to a new frequency, it feels great at first because it is a higher frequency of Love than you have previously accessed. Then as your body systems begin to release vibrations that do not resonate with it, there is a period of clearing and integration as these vibrations transform in the way that is perfect for you.

The releasing (or letting go of the "negative") is a vital part of establishing a new foundation of higher frequency. Do not resist this process; observe it and participate with it as your life path directs. Light Language will never throw someone into healing crisis because of the Higher Self filter that is inherent to it. However, if someone is extremely resistant to improvement, the Higher Self will initiate an opportunity for change. A person may be overly addicted to drama or use a healing crisis to reinforce an imbalanced ego of how unique or sensitive he or she is. Observe with detachment and learn how to interact with all types of people without losing your empowered balance.

Light Language often stirs issues that call you toward your empowerment.

Light Language often stirs issues that call you as a healer toward your empowerment as your Higher Self allows and activates the encodements. That is the nature of Love. Therefore, even if you are transmitting Light Language, you are receiving healing and expansion. It will affect your energy field for the better, just as it will for anyone you are working on. Yet some of the work depends on your action of choice to change. Though it is filtered through the Higher Self, Light Language does not remove your ability to participate and make new choices. The more you enhance your empowerment, the more you open to powerful flow. This results in Higher Self integration.

Enjoying Your Path

You will find that sharing Light Language with people who are seeking healing is a rewarding experience. One-on-one work is extremely valuable, both for you as you are growing your skills and confidence, and for the person receiving your focus. If healing others has no draw for you, your valuable service of healing yourself is changing the world. People often overlook the value of personal choices, but change only truly occurs on a broad scale when it occurs within each human being.

Observe your desires and be at peace with your path of change. Push beyond your fears at a pace that is just uncomfortable enough to strengthen you with relative ease. You will benefit greatly by nurturing yourself through change. Not everyone has the same path with Light Language, so observe yourself and see if you are pushing too much in a direction or not taking enough inspired action.

Light Language is an aspect of your expansion into what you already are, but from the perspective of the human form that is continuously progressing. You are becoming all that you already are. Again, the paradox. You are the I Am, becoming. You are powerful beyond what is currently visible and your biology is naturally available to your expansion. *Light Language can help gently and profoundly grow you into an expanded human state of being, communicating in ways that are both new to humanity and natural to humanity.* Enjoy your journey.

Chapter Thirty

Representing Light Language

It is important to remember that as you begin to transmit Light Language, you become a representative of it. With this, you wisely balance how you choose to expose others to it. How you exemplify it impacts all who are channeling Light Language. Spirit works in ways that are respectful of all involved, even though sometimes that moves people beyond their comfort zones.

Do not hide who you are, but be wise about how you can open another's heart to this beautiful and unique gift for humanity. Part of your work is embodying what empowerment is, knowing that all is well as it unfolds, and making choices that direct your path from the heart. Accept yourself as wise beyond scholastic degrees and valid beyond the recognition of others in ways that may not be accepted or as tangible. You are divinity in human form.

It is not your job to convince the world of the validity of Light Language and your healing gifts. Nor do you need to hide your gifts because other people don't understand or agree. It is your responsibility to help humanity Ascend into Love by living it yourself. Each person will have a unique pace and path.

Your Self-Respect and Courage

You have a responsibility as a healer to utilize Light Language for the highest good of All Life. Are you treating your clients with balanced empowerment? Are you honoring another's free will and asking permission appropriately? Are you taking care of yourself properly and nurturing yourself? Are you saying no when applicable and holding a loving, empowered boundary? Are you taking risks that move you beyond your comfort zone? Are you saying yes to the opportunities that support your growth? Are you honoring your needs and respecting when to charge an appropriate fee for your service or when to donate your time and skill?

I have met many people who represent Light Language respectfully. I have also met those who are steeped in ego imbalance and do not yet have the skill level that matches their price or offering. It is not that we must police Light Language; the energy emitted by a practitioner with integrity draws resonant experiences. Those who do not honor the Language of Light properly will have experiences that call them to their empowerment, Love, and new choice. It's not a punishment; it's a process of healing.

Observe with your own astute discernment of what is respectful to Light Language and to those who are yearning to experience it. Teach others integrity by your actions; respect yourself and others. Even if it isn't always a comfortable experience, respect is always a worthwhile choice.

Consideration of Others

How you represent Light Language and introduce others to it is an important responsibility. Humanity is learning to build and expand personal discernment and empowerment, as well as make a connection with its cosmic nature. Light Language is a bridge for this expansion, but it is not the only way you can discover it. Honor that there are many paths and some people may not be drawn to experience yours. Even if it seems like it, or another says it is about you; it is not personal—it's not about you. Your self-respect and courage within will allow you and others to have different experiences without judgment and hurt feelings.

Some seek to denigrate to feel comfortable, some seek to define in order to establish their own authority. Keep an open mind and heart, trust your discernment as to what is appropriate for you in a moment. It is important to keep an open mind and heart to positive and negative information flow while maintaining a neutrality that does not polarize toward or away from either. That is courageous work of balance and continued improvement

In these early stages of humanity's growing spiritual awareness, Light Language is an odd concept for many. Many people are not open to new things or feel uncomfortable with the open-ended experience of the conceptual nature of life. There is also still great fear and misunderstanding for many around channeling, both in known languages and Light Language. Empowered discernment is not available to everyone at this time.

If you accost someone with Light Language, you flavor their opinion of it. Is that a venue for the sacred? Could you help them more in that moment with a look of Love and a silent transmission that they are open to receive on the subtle planes because they haven't been shut down by such an odd and confusing experience? Could you ask them if they want to receive it and be well with their yes or no?

Mostly, those who are ready will come to you. There are so many people who are already open and drawn to Light Language, and this continues to expand exponentially. This is an exciting time in humanity's evolution. You will be sharing in ways that are best for the growth of your own courage and wisdom, as well as for others to receive it. Honor your path and continue to observe yourself for any ego imbalance that may have you pulling away or pushing too hard. This path of opening is about your authenticity, courage, patience, and practice.

HEALING EGO IMBALANCES

Observe yourself as you work to balance any fears or lack that may cause you to hide or seek attention. As humanity ascends into higher-dimensional frequencies, personal empowerment is key. Each being must build the internal discernment of what is valuable for his or her own development, healing, and path. Personal empowerment helps you make decisions that are beneficial for you, even if it is not always easy or looks different from another's path. Your clarity in all aspects of your life will strengthen your ability to channel and expand.

Working with the ego structure is a broad topic beyond the scope of this book. The ego is unique to each person and depends on his or her imbalance toward wanting attention or wanting to hide. One extreme over-validates the self, while the other extreme under-validates the self. Both require finding self-love and the strength to self-nurture rather than depending on outside sources to feed life force energy. Honest self-observance, Love, and nurturance are valuable practices that will benefit you greatly.

> *As a representative of Light Language, you serve this sacred communication as you exemplify integrity and honor.*

As you work with Light Language, you will naturally access energy that can help move you beyond these imbalances, but you must do your part of the work, too. Sometimes that is uncomfortable, like taking the risk to share Light Language with others. Sometimes it requires not needing attention and honoring others before yourself as you remain unnoticed in the moment.

Whatever your specific situation, Light Language will help you along that path. You will have experiences that strengthen you through support and opposition. Opposition need not be a horrible experience; let it be a challenge that strengthens you just as the negative YouTube comments I received caused me to self-observe, strengthen and understand others with a deeper compassion.

When you approach Light Language with the humility of honoring another's choice balanced with your confidence in your abilities, you find the grace of empowerment. With nothing to prove and nothing to force, you are open to honor any response with the empowerment of a master.

As you channel Light Language, you will enhance your own healing.

Balance your approach so you are continually excited and learning about Light Language. You will find that there is so much to experience and learn. You will find others who transmit it, and working with them can expand your own capabilities. You will be excited when you recognize or translate Languages from yourself and others. You will have thrilling experiences internally as you learn through the communication of your Higher Self. Allow it to unfold perfectly for you as you find the path that resonates with you.

Sacred Flow

Your path naturally calls you toward your empowerment, but you are the one who must choose to walk it. *As a representative of Light Language, you serve this sacred communication as you exemplify integrity and as you honor both your own and humanity's opening to it.* Your ethical standards are beneficial or detrimental to how others perceive the Language of Light. All it requires is doing the best you can in each moment. Continue to improve yourself, expand and learn. It's a fun and valuable journey.

As you channel Light Language, you will enhance your own healing. Practice often and observe yourself and others. Let the entire process be fascinating. If you find an ego imbalance in yourself, rejoice it! Now that you are aware of it, you can choose differently. The lack of awareness of ego imbalances is why many people cannot reliably create their reality.

You will constantly improve throughout life, so enjoy all aspects of your journey. The path of improvement can sometimes be frustrating, but you are so worth the effort. That climb of the high road is worth the panorama of broader perspective. Your life will look different as you open more to Light Language. Enjoy your progress.

Section Six

Light Language: Freedom Recognized

Universal Nature

Your universal nature is an important aspect of Light Language and Ascension. Humans are accustomed to perceiving the obvious separation of the earthly plane. Your senses, and even the ego structure, are the perfect apparatuses for earthly life. As humanity evolves beyond the separation of life, there is a natural progression into *connection*. Each individual becomes an empowered, strong, and Loving person, which changes the connectivity of the human species. There are wonderful clues in the nature of Light Language that help expand your connection into your universal nature.

Chapter Thirty One

The First Path

The first path of discovering your universal nature is recovering and healing parts of yourself so you are a strong, Loving **individual**. Becoming whole and empowered requires understanding the balance between strength and vulnerability. True strength requires vulnerability. You must stretch past your comfort zone to access your vulnerability, and then you must strengthen as you heal it. Realizing a vulnerability does not have to mean you will experience pain, but at times you may. Pain is often just a momentary experience of growth.

Light Language can help assist through this process as it initiates healing on a subconscious level through the agreement of the Higher Self. Yet it also induces a process of information opening that requires that you listen by reading the clues of your life.

As you become a whole and strong individual, change becomes easier. Forgiveness for yourself and others becomes easier. You find the strength to take the high road more often. You allow more easily because you know your ability to adapt and create a win-win out of any situation. You become more comfortable in your current life situation because you know you are capable of shifting it into something that continues to improve and delight you. You find yourself no longer feeling desperate for things like relationships, money or health. Instead, you begin to expect improvement because the current moment is merely a reaction to the past and it is supporting you to change. Empowerment and wonderment become your natural way of experiencing life, even when you have challenging moments.

> **The first path of discovering your universal nature is recovering and healing parts of yourself so you are a strong, Loving individual.**

Healing yourself and improving is a constant process. *It's not the drudgery of fixing what is broken, but the joy of evolution.* Light Language is a profound tool on this journey. Sometimes Lightworkers will avoid the negative by focusing on bliss. There is a misconception that unless you are blissful, something is wrong. Humanity is not yet at a state where monotone blissfulness is a functional reality. An *extremely* small percentage of people are meant to stay removed from day-to-day life and maintain a true blissful state. For most, polarizing to the positive is a state of avoidance. *However, integrating toward the positive is a balance of empowerment.* In that sense, positive doesn't mean the absence of all negative experiences, it means integrating toward Loving, empowering connection.

Sometimes people get tunnel vision about their belief systems and do not recognize when they are harboring anger, resentment or resistance to the processes of life. Life on Earth involves change, death and vulnerability. Yet it is all worth it, as it is balanced with creativity, birth, and strength. Your timeless, connected nature delves into Life with this Knowing. Observe your belief systems closely and determine if you are perceiving life and making choices that are based in your best interests, or if they are based in avoidance or righteousness. Only you can answer that for yourself. If a topic causes you an emotional reaction of resistance, you are out of balance with your perspective and energy toward it. It indicates that you have a vibrational opposition to it and that something needs to heal within you to attain your internal peace.

Mahatma Gandhi and Dr. Martin Luther King, Jr. are two wonderful examples of people who initiated positive change through extremely challenging circumstances. With two very difficult situations, they exemplified taking the high road of empowering resolution for all. They did not feel blissful Love at all times, but processed their anger into the wisdom of inspired action. This is the benefit of emotional authenticity and flow: it transforms.

Don't resist your authentic feelings. Allow them to teach you and move you beyond avoidance or resistance into wisdom integration. Light Language is a wonderful vehicle of wisdom flow and release that can help you adjust more easily. You will find more peace as you integrate your authentic negative reactions, emotions, and perspectives. If you find yourself feeling frustration at the process or the timing, work to shift your perspective into more detached observance. Find some fascination with the constant change of life and know your experience is leading you toward more balance and empowerment.

Being authentic in your thoughts and feelings is the key to moving past any negative emotions you harbor within—even ones you are not conscious of. Negative emotions are nothing more than indicators of resistance, fear or misunderstanding. When you let them flow into the integration of wisdom, you raise your vibration. Your new vibration gives you access to more peace, joy, freedom and creativity. You will be surprised at how rapidly you can improve, especially with the assistance of Light Language.

Chapter Thirty Two

The Second Path

Your empowered individuality leads to the second path of discovering your universal nature, though they also happen simultaneously. As you heal your internal emotional reactions to Life and become an empowered human, your vibration and your action choices begin to have a healing impact on others.

As you become empowered, you see that same potential in all others. As you love yourself, you feel love for others, even those you disagree with. As you initiate change through empowered choices, you change the track of humanity rather than continuing in opposition and suppression. Your balance with opposition and your loving courage to stand for beneficial change with Love in your heart is what brings real change—for you first, then for others.

Connecting and practicing with those who are similar to you can be wonderfully supportive. When you are able to connect with someone who is "opposite" of you, it begins your expansion into a fuller experience of your empowerment and the broader connected nature of Life. You know and live that all Life is from the same Source, equal in measure of Love and each with unique talents and focus. It can be wonderful practice to access this blissful state of connection in easier ways. Then you must observe yourself, stretch yourself and make sure you are integrating it practically with your life.

> *As you heal your internal emotional reactions to Life and become an empowered human, your vibration and your action choices begin to have a healing impact on others.*

For instance, can you go to work and remain mostly peaceful or blissful? Can you deal with family and maintain your state of Love? There are human Masters who seek opposition to determine their strength when appropriate, such as meditating in loud or offensive areas. When you can observe the human condition and feel empowering Love for it, you are strong enough to initiate deep improvement and progress here on Earth. In my own practice of improvement, I take that step by step without judgment of how I should be. I have an appreciation for awareness as it arises and a willingness to change, even if it takes time.

Feeling Love for a challenge doesn't mean it feels blissful, it means it feels like something that you know can change. The changing of it will be an exalting of wisdom and Love for humanity, not a forcing of acceptable behaviors. Light Language helps move you beyond the known of what has been before, into the potential that higher Love offers. This integrates a higher-dimensional expression for you, and ultimately for humanity. As you access the wisdom of Light Language, you discover potentials that become available from within you. You become a powerful catalyst for the improvement of life on Earth.

Light Language is an opportunity for rapid advancement as the wisdom of the heart penetrates the mind.

In order to help heal others by maintaining a high vibration, you are not required to be perfect. It only requires you to be balanced enough to assist another person with his or her challenges. Many healers have to deal with topics that would cause most people to reel in anger, hatred or engage in shaming. To maintain compassion in these instances is the only salve that will allow another person to balance into healing and empowerment.

The days when a healer can be out of balance in day-to-day life and assist others are diminishing. It will become increasingly difficult for humanity to remain polarized and repress internal pain. This is due to the vibration of the collective raising into a greater expanse of Love. You may not see it in the media, but it is occurring. Adults are making more loving and empowering choices for themselves and others. Children incarnate already vibrating with great Love, and now that Love is better able to anchor here on Earth. It is an exciting time for the evolution of humanity. *Light Language is an opportunity for rapid advancement as the wisdom of the heart penetrates the mind.*

You are a vital part of the evolution of humanity and you are affecting the collective vibration with every choice you make. This is why it is so important to heal your emotional and mental imbalances and bring your vibration into one of authentic balance and empowerment. This shifts what is available to others who may not yet have the courage or awareness to heal their own issues. Your adaptability and balance offer the possibility of healing to others. Continuing repression or avoidance maintains a strong availability of that vibration here on Earth.

This correlates with the interesting phenomenon of disinformation or obsessive focus on conspiracy theories. When a human chooses to use the power of their Light for hatred against governments, corporations or institutions, it continues that energy dominance. It is perfectly natural and valuable to observe what humanity is doing wrong (harming) and even feel negative feelings about it. Just don't continue the focus on what is wrong. Implement new perspective, forgiveness and inspired action. *Change the vibration.* As you do this, you shift your own vibrational signature and the collective resonance. Those who have a life path of changing the physical systems of humanity (like governments or medical care) will find that indicated by their inspired action. It's not always easy, and certainly not blissful in general; but these people are compelled to act and their actions create change for the greater good. Your Loving vibration helps them do their work.

Entrainment is a physical phenomenon wherein two or more separate vibrating systems, like two tuning forks or two humans, begin to naturally shift their vibrations to the same frequency. A higher vibration will slow and the lower (slower) vibration will increase. This is why it is important to have a genuinely balanced vibration. *If you are avoiding reality to keep your vibration at a higher frequency, you will be easily dragged down by the lower vibrations around you.*

For example, Jesus maintained a powerfully Loving vibration even in the face of the worst aspects of humanity. That is why people experienced such profound healings around him, and why he cautioned them with the (paraphrased) advice, "Don't talk to others about this healing." He knew they were strengthening their own vibration after meeting with him, and could have undone their healing by allowing others to judge or criticize it before they were strong enough to maintain it.

If you have a strong, empowered, higher-vibrating frequency that has been created by healing your issues, you will maintain it more readily and raise people up to yours, even as you notice the uncomfortable feeling of the vibrational difference. Light Language helps you transmute negativity into wisdom, just as it helps your physical body maintain a healthier resonance. It's only part of the formula, though, as you must make empowered choices when change is necessary.

The community aspect of Life is part of your universal nature. This is the equivalent of respecting yourself and all others as appropriate. In this way, you observe the vibrational potential of when it is appropriate to stand up against another and speak with honesty, when it is appropriate to say nothing or when to disengage from a relationship. Those answers vary by the situation and the moment. There is never a mistake. Any choice that results in an uncomfortable situation or tears is not a mistake; it is a clearing of energy and a lesson learned. Sometimes saying nothing is appropriate while in another instance saying nothing is avoidance. Even avoidance is merely a choice in the moment that can result in a lesson learned, so have no judgment about it. Avoidance is a survival mechanism that can be beneficial until one is strong enough to handle change. There are no mistakes, only experiences.

As you open your perspective to the empowering potential of yourself and others, you interact with the subtle realms of possibility and make choices that serve improvement. *You become adept at participating in the shaping of Life on Earth rather than reacting to problems.* It is a powerful choice that in the moment may or may not be fulfilling, for manifestation typically takes time to form. However, you will begin to receive clues of the impending manifestation.

You are empowering yourself, creating your life, and offering hope and emulation to others. *Humanity begins to change because you are changing yourself.* As you open to Light Language, you open to great potentials of change. This powerful catalyst can elevate you vibrationally, intellectually and creatively. It helps you change your life for the better.

Chapter Thirty Three

The Third Path

This brings us to the third aspect of integrating your universal nature. *Love becomes your natural state and you connect into Life beyond the beautiful reality currently manifested on Earth.* You become aware of heart-centered information in every situation that supports the beauty of Life and the potential of all of humanity's transformation. It elevates you to create the life of your dreams, even if the details are different than you thought they would be.

In this state of empowered Love, you find that your universal nature and power are stronger than any lack or fear. You discover the potentials hidden in plain sight. You understand that it is as easy as being open to Love in all its facets. You see the gifts in challenge and triumph alike because each situation leads to improvement. You become better able to manifest improvement as you open to potentials with less resistance to "problems." Miracles of all kinds begin to align with you (synchronicities). However, you aren't doing it for the manifestations, you're doing it for the Love of Life.

You begin to tap into your galactic, angelic, and/or elemental nature more. There is no resistance of being human upon it, just a natural opening of knowing you are vast, wise and human. There is not an overwhelming longing for home, merely a Loving of home, because it truly is wherever your heart is, wherever your focus is. Light Language is a bridge of communication between your self in human form and your Higher Self, which is in subtle form and connected with All Life. Your vastness becomes revealed.

You open to abilities and experiences that make being human an expansive experience. You have a greater ability to define the cycles and symbols of life and the entire puzzle becomes play. You find the wonderment of your inner child integrated with the wisdom of your timeless inner master. The universe itself is home to you. Your universal nature is natural. That is the power of Love.

Love becomes your natural state and you connect into Life beyond the beautiful reality currently manifested on Earth.

Light Language can be a valuable part of integrating your universal nature. As you allow a safe and vast connection beyond the typical human experience and apply it into the human experience, Life expands. It is possible to remain grounded and loving in this reality and integrate higher-dimensional expression. Indeed, it is the only way to truly change this experience on Earth.

As you embrace who you are in human form and integrate who you are in universal form (subtle, connected, vast, timeless), you elevate your frequency and emanate new potential to all you meet. Life is changing because of you. You are so worth the journey.

Conclusion

When I began discovering my spiritual nature, I never anticipated my life would take the path of opening to Light Language. At times I had to be shown that I had the courage by loving, invisible guidance that pushed me past my comfort zone and comforted me into my empowerment zone. I also found the support of friends who were having similar experiences or who were supportive in other ways, as well as those human angels who supported me through beneficial opposition.

My experience with Light Language and channeling have shown me parts of the nature of Life, and even myself, that I never would have imagined possible. My life is sometimes magical, mundane or frustrating, but I appreciate all of it because it keeps me expanding. Now even the frustrating parts are indicators of change and opportunity that I appreciate along the way. I continue to be amazed at the ability to expand beyond what I knew before, to meet others who expand me, and to help others expand as well.

As I recognized that Life is always working for me, not against me, I began to open to my natural peace and courage to flow more easily and boldly with life. It tested and developed my patience and focus. I have never stopped my healing process, because I have never stopped learning and growing. I continue to open to new Languages and abilities, which may happen for you, too.

As a Lightworker, you work directly with the Light of Love within each human, *beginning with yourself.* You open to new abilities and interact with higher dimensions as you integrate more Love in your life. You create a path for others to emulate and modify for their own needs and desires. You are part of the process of raising the vibration of humanity such that evolution speeds and eases for many. Light Language is a bridge, part of the connection of humanity.

What we are moving through is a deepening of our understanding between separation and connection, the two opposites of this human experience. Through the lens of Light Language, we can begin to understand linearity and its immersion in non-linearity, the mirror that we are. We bridge universal law into the physical with a grounded understanding and application within the rules of our density. That embodiment changes our subtle structures and then our physical structures over time. There are broader layers of connection to Light Language that will unfold with actual resonance shift, as the veil of separation gives way to greater connection. The mist clears and what was unseen becomes known through experience. Then the next invisible layer begins to reveal itself.

My hope for you is that you also find the magic of Life in each moment and that Light Language is a fulfilling aspect of your expansion. You are complete and ever-expanding, perfect and ever-changing. You embody the paradox of being Divine in human form. Enjoy your powerful journey. I honor your courage. I honor your Light.

Thank you for taking this journey with me.

Stay Connected with Jamye

The best way to stay connected with Jamye is to subscribe to her private mailing list. Here she shares information that she doesn't share publicly, because it is for those that are serious about more in-depth information on their path of Ascension. It contains all that she shares publicly so you have access to any new videos, Light Language transmissions, classes or products available.

Receive Jamye's latest videos and articles to assist your spiritual path of empowerment.

Visit JamyePrice.com and subscribe today!

Join a powerful community of change!

Glossary

Akashic Records are the extensive, multidimensional library of the history of humankind through Earth incarnations and lifecycles on other planets and dimensions. They are etheric and accessible through our Lightbody functionality and DNA.

All of Life—When capitalizations are used beyond normal grammatical application, it denotes a broader definition of the term. Life and All of Life expand the definition of life beyond a human living and dying, or beyond the scientific model of a living organism. All of Life refers to all consciousness on Earth, beyond Earth, and even beyond the physical plane.

Areon, the Lyran Council of Time, is a loving group of beings from Lyra that are communicating through Jamye to assist humanity with Ascension. Their focus is the mental and emotional aspects of Ascension that empower beings to be authentically loving and change this Earth experience by first changing internally—where true change begins.

Ascension is a natural evolutionary process of improvement. At this stage in human development, it is focused on greater understanding and interaction with the subtle, unseen realms of existence. Just as the microscope provided insight into the unseen realm, humans are evolving into understanding their own natural biomechanism that interacts with the unseen.

This begins with an understanding of subatomic structures and frequency, then stretches into intuition and connection. Spirit and science begin to connect, and humanity expands understanding and utilization of a natural functionality.

Atlantis is an ancient reference noted in some of Plato's work. It is claimed as legend by some and reality by others. There is some historical evidence to support a real culture that Plato referred to; however, there is no official agreement as to the specifics. Atlantis is believed to be an advanced civilization that succumbed to a love of power and eventually sank into the ocean.

Auric Field is the space around your body that contains your aura. This is an electromagnetic field and is truly an extension of your physical body in another frequency range. People call this many things and differentiate it on many different levels: causal body, Ka body, energetic field, etc. It is a wonderful indicator of many different aspects of a person: health, disposition, integrity. The aura changes frequently.

Axiatonal Alignment—Your body has a grid system within it known as the meridian system that flows energy (as taught in Eastern medicine). Your body also has a grid system within the auric field known as the axiatonal system that flows energy. The axiatonal system connects us to an intricate and interdimensional grid system that is universal in nature. Activating this system will help flow higher frequencies into your physical body. This brings you into alignment with your universal purpose and revitalizes your connection with the entirety of you.

Crystalline Soul Healing® is a modality that Jamye developed through work with her non-physical Guide Team over many years. It is about Soul Progression—rapid, deep, joyful change and ascension. It works deeply with the soul. Crystalline Soul Healing assists with removing vibrational data in the field that is blocking the client from the clear perfection of who they are. All beings are all perfect, just in need of some balance at times. Sometimes an issue shifts quickly, sometimes it takes more of a learning process for the client, yet it is always perfect. This modality helps you step into the fullness of yourself so that you are living heaven on earth, and holding the power of Love within you so that you are emitting the Love frequency for yourself and those that need it. Crystalline Soul Healing is about helping you along that journey—the journey that changes the world. Visit JamyePrice.com to learn more about it or become a practitioner.

Dharma is a term with many different interpretations and definitions. I define it as your ultimate path of service. For instance, if someone is a wonderful nurturer, then becoming a parent, teacher, or doctor may be his or her dharma.

Divine Light is the divinity inherent within all life, especially you. Your love is like a candle in the night, illuminating love. Each being has an equal amount of Divine Light, or divinity, within. Yet not every person is acting from divinity in each moment. The more clarity, courage, and balance you have determines whether you are acting (or reacting) from your divinity or your fear and insecurity. As you become an empowered sovereign being, you learn to live life from your Divine Light. This is the path of Ascension humanity is embarking on, activating more of the Divine Light that is inherent within. This changes your physical body, how you interact emotionally and mentally, and even how you process light, which contains information.

DNA Activation is a broad term that is often misunderstood. DNA is the instruction set the body uses within each cell to replicate and continue your life. It has a wide range of functionality unknown to conventional science, but that is apparent through the evidence of what some beings can achieve, like psychic senses, rejuvenation, brain functionality, and more. The term "DNA activation" refers to making these dormant functionalities accessible. While that does happen by receiving energy healing or activations from someone, the core of it is really about your own journey of improvement. For example, each time you forgive, hold a healthy boundary for yourself, or take a creative risk, you are activating your DNA. When you release pain, love yourself, or take loving, courageous actions, you are shifting the instruction set your body uses to replicate information in your body.

Encodements are information. Light Language is vast with information that your Higher Self activates. Information and encodements are used interchangeably throughout this book. The word encodements helps you realize that beyond the "words" that are flowing is rich and multilayered vibrational data.

Free Will is your internal choice of how you deal with all experiences in your life. You have complete control over your internal responses, though you must grow the skill of not being controlled by outside circumstances. As you release fears and insecurities, you naturally grow your ability to access your inner empowerment with all circumstances you encounter. You have free will with your actions as well; however, part of your external experiences is a co-creation with life. For example, you do not have the free will to disregard the laws of your country without consequence. Humanity resides in a conditional realm of physical existence and it will be naturally integrated and moved beyond. Therefore, as you respond to the laws of humans with neutrality, you are integrating your empowerment and your internal peace (with paying taxes, for example). This strengthens you into access with higher-frequency information, experiences, and beingness. In this way, the "limitations" of your free will are not a barrier to your progress; they are a structure within which you thrive and expand.

Guides (along with **Guide Team**) refers to nonphysical energies that assist a being in his or her knowledge and development. *Guides communicate in many ways and need not be heard directly.* Your Higher Self is always a Guide and always acts as the filter for all you experience. A balanced ego is imperative to filter experiences that are not based in Love. When your ego is not balanced, you are open to information and manipulation from beings that do not have your best interest at heart. Your Higher Self supports your human journey of free will and progress through experience. Because your Higher Self is eternal in nature, it unconditionally allows you experience and also conditionally directs you in experience that is in alignment with your soul intention. If your intention is Love-based, you will experience challenge and triumph that supports that. If your intention is ego-based, you will experience energy that is in alignment with that as well. Your clarity and empowerment are key to accessing the information of Guides that resonate with a high frequency of Love.

Higher Self is the aspect of you that exists in a frequency range beyond the physical senses or the physical body. It is you in the subtle, unseen state of connection and omniscient awareness. It is the higher-frequency aspect of you. It is not bound by linear timespace; therefore, it is timeless (residing in all time) and resides in all space—within you, outside of you, close to you, and far away from you. Your Higher Self is limitless, and like all of the subtle, invisible realm, it is much vaster than the physical part of you. Just as the atomic structure is approximately ninety-nine percent space and one percent matter, so too are your Higher Self and you. The process of Ascension increases your vibration (frequency) in the physical realm of life, thereby raising it to a closer resonance with the Higher Self. This raises the collective of humanity into a fourth-density vibration (sometimes referred to as fourth- or fifth-dimensional expression). Ascension is about accessing more connective, Loving perspectives, which integrates your Higher Self with you more readily. Every being that is alive is connected to his or her Higher Self. How conscious you are determines how actively connected you are to your Higher Self. When you are interacting from unconscious, fear-based responses, you are not utilizing a frequency that is closer to the high-frequency Higher Self. Because your Higher Self knows you are a brilliant spiritual being in human form, it will allow and encourage experiences that have a potential to strengthen you into understanding your Loving nature. These experiences may foster choices for forgiveness, self-love, and many other opportunities to choose a Loving vibration.

I Ching is superficially known as a divination tool; however, it is much more than that. It is an ancient Chinese system of understanding and utilizing the natural movement and properties of life. It began as a whole line and a broken line, representing a yes and a no, respectively. It then became a collection of sixty-four combinations of whole and broken lines. Each of these combinations represent properties of existence and the moving through the changes of existence.

Kundalini is the dormant energy that is awakened through spiritual practice. Like a fire, it burns off the dross that keeps you perceiving mainly through the physical senses and opens you to a higher frequency range of perception. In Hindu traditions it is considered to be stored in the sacrum and spirals up the spine when initiated. The effects range from physical, emotional, and mental experiences that create a purification of the being, sometimes in uncomfortable and potentially challenging ways. Certain activities, like Light Language, can activate the kundalini, though it is a detailed practice. Meditation is generally the best practice, as it typically activates the kundalini at a manageable pace.

Lemuria is an ancient civilization that resided on Earth approximately 50,000 years ago; little remnants of it remain in physical view. It sank prior to the sinking of Atlantis, so much of the Lemurian structures are now either below sea level or have been merged with later cultures. There is no agreed-upon mainstream historical proof of the existence of Lemuria.

Lightbody is the etheric structure that transduces frequencies of light and sound from subtle to dense (physical) and their effects on the person. It contains different subtle structures that support your physical thriving and connection with the subtle realms. It contains the chakra system, the Djed column, the Merkaba, and the Axiatonal system. It is the invisible structure that accesses or holds the information of the Akashic Records, karmic propensities, and emotional/mental signatures. This multidimensional structure is both outside and within the physical body and acts as a receiver of resonant energy and a deflector of non-resonant frequencies.

Lightworker—All humans are potential Lightworkers. This definition pertains to those choosing to consciously improve the experience of life on Earth through Love. A Lightworker consciously chooses a path of self-improvement and one of improving life on Earth. This path of progress requires active participation in choosing Love over shame, blame, repression, or unconscious behavior. It is often confused with only experiencing the pleasant things in life. On the contrary, it indicates a deep courage to experience the full spectrum of life and integrate it into empowered Love.

Multidimensional pertains to multiple dimensions, dimensional expressions, or densities. Within the context of this book it denotes an application beyond the dimensions that are available to our physical senses. This offers access into information and experience that is beyond the limits of time and space in our physical density.

Polarity refers to a division to opposite extremes. Human life is often referred to as a duality experience because most things separate into two opposites, such as male/female, us/them, me/you, good/bad, etc. Polarity Integration is the merging of these opposites within yourself and your perceptions, which begins a path of wholeness rather than separation. Polarity Integration is Ascension, releasing any fears or insecurities that keep you avoiding an opposite frequency (for example, polarizing to focus only on love without resolving anger within), and accessing your courage of Love to integrate an opposite into understanding, compassion, and new choice.

Soul braids describe the Higher Self integrating within the physical experience once the physical body has risen to a new frequency setpoint. As you release lower-density vibrations like fear, shame, blame, or insecurities, you are raising your vibration. As you choose self-love, Love others, forgive, or hold a healthy boundary, you are raising your vibration. This allows aspects of you that reside in a higher frequency to merge into your physical experience. This is a natural process of Ascension. It is sometimes referred to as an incarnational overlay or a Higher Self overlay.

Soul Progression is about stepping into Ascension and making a decision to move your emotional, mental, physical, and spiritual evolution forward. It's a pathway to enlightenment that is different for every person and will result in learning who you are on a soul level and bringing that into your physicality. It requires releasing any vibratory data that is not resonant with a high frequency of Love. It requires actions that entrain you to a higher frequency. This evolves your physicality by resolving vibrational discord into understanding. It is your evolution as a sovereign being.

Soul groups are groups of resonant beings that are working through karmic evolution together. They have intertwining experiences that are a necessary reflection for progress. For instance one person from your soul group may be a great loving supporter who strengthens you, while another may be a perpetrator who strengthens you. Because the supporters feel so good, you tend to recognize them more easily.

Throughout linear time on Earth, we refine our soul streams. This means you may have had past lives where you were blended with others in your soul group.

Source/Divine Source is the same as God, the Creator of All That Is, Love, or any other term a person or a religion may use to refer to the One Source of Life or the connection of Life.

Telepathic Communication generally refers to a thought being transferred directly to another mind. I expand this definition into an intuitive understanding, incorporating the full empathic capabilities of receiving information through thought, emotion, physical sensation, or clairvoyant imagery. The human system has an intuitive sense for every physical sense, so you can even receive telepathic smells, tastes, sounds, temperatures and more.

Tree of Life is a universal symbol recognized and used in some form by most religions throughout the world. The Tree of Life symbol utilized in Kabbalah contains a physical structure that represents the properties of human existence and how these properties interact.

Walk-In refers to a person whose original soul is replaced by another. This process is less necessary now because humanity's frequency has increased enough to accommodate access to higher-frequency aspects of self and life. Quite often this would occur during an accident. It is often associated with spirituality because it generally occurs to allow for spiritual evolution or karmic resolution.

Yuga is an epoch or era that comprises long cycles of time. This relates to the cycles of humanity's consciousness as it expands and contracts in concurrence with the larger time cycles Earth exists within. Many ancient traditions track these larger time cycles accurately, though there is also some disagreement as to the exact timing and implications of them. These cycles can be tracked into our galaxy's alignment with the galactic center, and observed through our zodialogical signs through this longer time cycle of alignment with the galactic center. In essence, we see smaller cycles within larger cycles, and these all have information that is beneficial to observe.

BIBLIOGRAPHY

Lyssa Royal Holt and Keith Preist, *The Prism of Lyra*. Light Technology Publishing, Second Edition 2011.

Jamie Sams, *Sacred Path Cards: The Discovery of Self Through Native Teachings*. Harper Collins, 1990.

Vianna Stibal, *Theta Healing: Introducing an Extraordinary Energy Healing Modality*. Hay House, 2011.

Lee Carroll, *The Kryon Series of Books*. The Kryon Writings, Inc., 1993 – 2015

University of Pennsylvania, The measurement of regional cerebral blood flow during glossolalia: A preliminary SPECT study. Andrew B. Newberg, Nancy A. Wintering, Donna Morgan, Mark R. Waldman

J.J. Hurtak, The Book of Knowledge: The Keys of Enoch. The Academy for Future Sciences, Fourth Edition, 1999

Michael Talbot, The Holographic Universe: The Revolutionary Theory of Reality. Harper Perennial, Reprint Edition, 2011.

Masaru Emoto, The Hidden Messages in Water. Atria Books, 2005.

Hans Jenny, Cymatics: A Study of Wave Phenomena & Vibration. MACROmedia Publishing, Third Edition, 2001.

J. R. R. Tolkien, The Lord of the Rings Trilogy. Houghton Mifflin Harcourt; Anniversary Edition, 2007.
— The Hobbit, Anniversary Edition, 2007.
— The Lord of the Rings, Anniversary Edition, 2007.
— The Fellowship of the Rings, Anniversary Edition, 2007.

Bruce Lipton, Biology of Belief: Unleashing the Power of Consciousness, Matter, & Miracles. Hay House, Revised Edition, 2008.

The Bible, John, 14:12, NKJV

Haramein, N., Rauscher, E.A., and Hyson, M. (2008). Scale Unification: A Universal Scaling Law. Proceedings of the Unified Theories Conference. ISBN 9780967868776; http://resonance.is/explore/publications/

Andrew Zimmerman Jones, Young's Double Slit experiment http://physics.about.com/od/lightoptics/a/doubleslit.htm

Rene Peoc'h Research, http://www.retrouverson-nord.be/poussin_robot_these_peoch.pdf

Christian Huygens Research, http://www-history.mcs.st-and.ac.uk/Biographies/Huygens.html

Buckminster Fuller Research, https://bfi.org/

Bibliography

Nassim Haramein Research, http://resonance.is/

Gariaev/ Poponin Research; The Phantom DNA Effect, http://www.emergentmind.org/gariaev06.htm

Star Trek and related marks are trademarks of CBS Studios Inc.

Star Wars and related marks are trademarks of Lucasfilm, Ltd.

Tools for Ascension

Jamye's passion is Ascension and providing you *practical* esoteric information and processes to assist you on your unique journey.

Visit JamyePrice.com for tools to transform your life!

- Learn Light Language online
- Become a Crystalline Soul Healing® practitioner
- Cosmic Consciousness Ascension Deck
- Light Language audio programs
- Powerful teleclasses and channelings
- Online classes for personal growth
- Retreats and intensives with Jamye
- Videos and articles

Embrace your Light and shine it brilliantly!

Praise for Jamye's Light Language Classes

Visit JamyePrice.com to find out if a class is right for you

"The ease and grace in which it flowed was amazing. No gaps in the presentation for us to get confused or feel lost AT ALL. The material effortlessly built upon itself to give us a full comprehensive experience in all ways. I loved your humor and willingness to address questions with such patience, love and WISDOM!!"

"I have never attended any event that presented the material so succinctly and so thoroughly."

"The environment that she has created in the class is so safe and supportive. The fear just melts away."

"I had tried a couple of other teachers prior to this that have classes on CD or DVD. It's nothing like this intensive class. This was incredible. This provided the structure I needed to learn how to speak it, write it and sign it."

"It was life change and healing. It's like I've jumped to a higher level. I can feel that I've progressed to a new step that I can apply into my one-on-one contact with people."

"The way she presents each progression of exercises opens you up a little bit more. I feel that confidence that it will progress even more."

"Such a glorious environment of trust, respect, support and openness was created."

"I was so drawn to Jamye's grounded presence, her authenticity and her way of bringing to us such sacred and important learning in a way that is accessible. She uses humor and shares her own experiences to help us realize the light language is accessible to all of us who are willing to open our hearts, receive and transmit. Jamye is the most genuine, real and truly gifted teacher I've encountered in a long while. It is a rare thing to see a teacher balance humility and purity of message. "

"Just gratitude. I've witnessed so much change in me in a few days' time. Looking forward to seeing how much greater life is. I feel more open to receive the blessings that are my birthright"

Crystalline Soul Healing

"It's been two weeks and I already see the changes. I feel my back is healing. I feel more confident and unconsciously I'm aware of my self worth."

"For a long time I would have these random very negative thoughts which I never could truly relate to. After our session the thoughts are gone. The feeling of something stuck in the back of my throat is completely gone. It was bruised feeling for a few days but now totally gone."

"Hi Jamye, I just wanted to tell you that I truly believe the last session we had together was the start of the change for everything for me. Thank you so much."

"Jamye, since our sessions I've had some amazing transformation. I don't use the word amazing lightly. I have lost 13.8 lbs in 14 days (normally fast loss not healthy, in this case very healthy), I have more real energy (not adrenal driven) and am sleeping better than I have in 20 years. My work in the world is transforming in unexpected ways. My marriage has had a break-through in a wonderful way. Most important I am absolutely well – happy, filled with a clarity and peace that I have not felt in my being since, well, I do not remember."

Cosmic Consciousness Ascension Deck

"I really REALLY love this deck. I have been reading Oracle and Tarot of all kinds for 20 years and this is one of the most unique and finely tuned instruments I have come across. There is no divination here necessarily just pure divine assistance and I love it."

"I was at a point of feeling stuck and not knowing how to proceed to create change. With the cards and your website, I feel I have been given much needed tools that are helping me in a very practical and effective way to work with thoughts, beliefs and patterns and to allow change more easily. I feel more balanced and supported and I'm trusting life more. I'm so thankful!"

"These are the most amazing cards, that continue to blow my spiritual conscious mind to the next level"

"I love this deck! I have been using for myself as well as I did a short mini read for a friend and was right on for both of us! The book that comes with it is so spot on. The messages are so clear and concise."

"They are amazing, and brought lots of interest with my three kids, even my husband was very attracted!! It feels very safe to work with and grounded in the same time even if it is stars related!"

"I received my card deck yesterday and the book! It is the first card deck I have ever purchased. (Just so you know). I have been totally moved to tears by the meaning that is emanating from the cards I have pulled and from the book. The palpable high vibration of the cards feels like something new has come into my world that is totally resonant for me at this point in time. I can feel that this information contains within it a lot of healing and new growth for me. In awe!"

"I have found them to be very powerful in that they have their own consciousness. Each card I draw tells a story in a simple yet profound way that helps clarify questions I have."

"It offers me exactly what I need at the right times and it has been a treasure to me beyond words. Thank you."

Light Language Healing Audios

"I have seen amazing results already. My psoriasis has been flaring up for the last few years. I have tried everything. My friend suggested this. It is working. The red scaly patches are lighter and smoother. I wish I had taken before and after pictures."

———————————

"Thank you Jamye. Several issues have improved for me since I found your website. The Sacred Relationship guided meditation is one of the best I've encountered in 25 years. It helps me clear my chakras and release stress."

———————————

"How amazing it is. I alternated days between the meditation and the light language. I felt a new sense of calm I had not felt before. The light language, sticks with me."

———————————

"I love your work, although sometimes, I have to stop because the shifts are too much! Not a complaint, just an observation."

———————————

"I wanted to express my gratitude for all I received from you. I'm working with your Healing recordings, and it's so wonderful to see certain things are no longer in my space; I feel more and more free and empowered. Thank you so much!"

———————————

"I started listening through all your programs once again. I noticed that new layers are releasing, and they get much deeper this time around. I love the energy!"

———————————

Classes

"Thank you so much for such a beautiful and powerful class! I could feel myself becoming even more open."

"I have been doing the Pineal exercise and finding that I am feeling different. It's a good thing! I can feel it!"

"I must say it was the perfect timing for me. It worked well and the energy transmissions pushed me in a very interesting state."

"I have attended all your tele-sessions this year and they were such a powerful tool. The timing of your themes (tele-sessions, newsletters and weekly light-blasts) that you have presented and interpreted during the past months, is almost mind boggling in its precision and accuracy."

"Thank you so much for your such a transformative, beautiful class last night! The truth is, I have been feeling completely at the bottom of everything in my life lately. This morning, I woke up completely feeling different. I feel my life is fine. The strongest experience for me last night was, I literally felt a blockage was shot out of my heart."

More information available at JamyePrice.com

About the Author

Jamye Price, author of *The Cosmic Consciousness Ascension Deck*, is an international energy healer, channel, and teacher. She developed a healing modality, Crystalline Soul Healing, a powerful alchemical template for Soul Progression. In addition, Jamye channels healing energies in the form of Light Language, which are transformational Creation Codes that further align you with your Soul. She teaches both of these modalities worldwide.

Jamye also channels Areon, of the Lyran Council of Time. These loving Lyran messages are focused on humanity's Ascension and connecting you with your timeless nature as humanity moves into fourth and fifth dimensional expression. As a universal, full-body channel Jamye is able to channel many loving beings that are aligned with assisting the Ascension of humanity.

Jamye has been facilitating healing sessions and classes for over a decade. Her work assists with transmuting physical, emotional, mental and spiritual blocks into wisdom, compassion and empowerment. She teaches self-love, forgiveness and finding a perspective of Love in any situation to provide people with practical tools for Soul Progression and creating a joyful life. With Crystalline Soul Healing, Light Language, and an open channel to loving guidance that is specific to an individual, she is able to help people change their life rapidly.

For more information visit JamyePrice.com

Printed in Great Britain
by Amazon